"Today is the 'day of the saints.' I can't think of a [...] release more than fifty percent of souls into the mi[...] could be revolutionary for the Church of the 21st century."

Dr. Che Ahn, senior pastor, Harvest Rock Church, Pasadena

"A great company of women is being raised up by the Lord in this hour to proclaim the Gospel. This company will carry the fragrance of Jesus, the humility of the Spirit, the might of the Lion of the tribe of Judah and will comfortably take its place in the Body of Christ. Shirley Sustar not only paints the vision of this holy call but blows the trumpet concerning the need for mentoring those who are being raised up. 'Where have all the mothers gone?' *Become a Woman of Power* will bring challenge, encouragement and faith to all who read its pages."

Patricia King, Extreme Prophetic

"Brilliantly written, *Become a Woman of Power* is filled with heartfelt lessons from a personal journey mingled with biblical insight to reach today's women right where they live. Shirley Sustar helps clothe Christ's royal woman with security in Him and calls them forth into their divine destinies. A great tool for mentoring!"

James W. and Michal Ann Goll, cofounders, Encounters Network; authors, *The Seer and Women on the Frontlines*

"Because of the devil's fear of women, he has inspired men to develop customs and religious teaching to keep women subjugated in a lesser role than God ordained for them. This book will be instrumental in raising up a company of mighty women of power who will be set free and activated by the truth and special mentoring. Let God's anointed women arise and crush the head of Satan!"

Dr. Bill Hamon, chairman and founder, Christian International Ministries Network; president, Christian International Business Network

"The Church of Jesus Christ is in a season of unprecedented release as women seize their God-given purposes. *Become a Woman of Power* will prove to be a tool to bring women, ministry and the Church together toward this goal and toward the end-time harvest of souls."

Mike Bickle, director, International House of Prayer of Kansas City

"Revelatory, challenging and much needed in the Body of Christ today. Thank you for your insight and openness to share with us and help us get on the right track!"

Dr. Pam Rutherford, Set Free Evangelistic Ministries

"Many young women are crying out for mentors. Who will arise to answer that cry, and what will the mentor say and do? This book speaks clearly about both issues with scriptural and practical answers. Shirley has done a great job with this subject. Get this book and study it."

Barbara J. Yoder, Michigan state coordinator, United States Strategic Prayer Network; National Apostolic Council, United States Strategic Prayer Network

"One of the most critical tasks facing the Church is the task of nurturing, developing, disciplining and mentoring believers. The Body of Christ desperately needs committed servants who will partner with God toward the type of positive change that brings us closer to what God intends for our lives. God has raised up 21st-century midwife Shirley Sustar to inspire every daughter in the Kingdom to reproduce spiritual life."

The Rev. Gina M. Stewart, pastor, Christ Missionary Baptist Church, Memphis

"The need for spiritual mothers in the Church today should be apparent to all. Older women must be released to do what God has called them to do. *I like this book!* I can't wait to see it in the hands of many pastors, leaders and women of all ages."

Prophet **Lattie McDonough**, McDonough Ministries

"Through practical situations, transparency and personal examples, Shirley helps women relate to the heart issues God is after in every woman willing to pay the price. I believe it is a timely word for the Body of Christ. *Become a Woman of Power* has encouraged me and spurred me with new insight and revelation for my own life and church."

Carol Hilbrant, co-pastor, Elsinore Christian Center, Lake Elsinore, Calif.

"As you read this book, your eyes will be opened to new things in God. You will be encouraged and affirmed in the insights you are already walking out. And you will find a renewed desire to pick up the torch and finish the race. Where were you, Shirley, when I was first trying to grow up in God? Your practical way of communicating God's desires for women's lives gives insight and inspiration and cuts the time it takes for us to discover these things for ourselves. Thank you for saying so clearly the things that need to be said to encourage us to rise to a higher level in Him because of His love and the high calling on our lives."

Vivian Cunningham, co-pastor, Rancho Christian Center, Rancho Cucamonga, Calif.

"Shirley Sustar writes from experience, not just theory. Having experienced our own spiritual development through mentoring under the hand of both her and her husband, we have grown from spiritual infancy to spiritual parenthood and are now doing the same."

Daryl and Debbie Snyder, Balkan regional directors, Apostolic Team Ministries; senior pastors, Bashkesia E Ungillit, Velore, Albania

BECOME
A WOMAN OF
POWER

*Releasing Mighty Women of God
through Mentoring*

Shirley Sustar

Chosen
Grand Rapids, Michigan

Published by Chosen Books
a division of Baker Publishing Group
P.O. Box 6287, Grand Rapids, MI 49516-6287
www.chosenbooks.com

Printed in the United States of America

Library of Congress Cataloging-in-Publication Data
Sustar, Shirley.
    Become a woman of power : releasing mighty women of God through mentoring / Shirley Sustar.
        p.   cm.
    ISBN 0-8007-9391-9 (pbk.)
    1. Christian women—Religious life. 2. Mentoring in church work. I. Title.
BV4527.S86 2005
248.8′43—dc22   2004022976

Unless otherwise noted, Scripture is taken from the Amplified® Bible, Copyright © 1954, 1958, 1962, 1964, 1965 by The Lockman Foundation. Used by permission.

Scripture marked KJV is taken from the King James Version of the Bible.

Information on pp. 69–70 is used by permission The Voice of the Martyrs www.persecution .com.

To my mother, Alice Lacas,
who dedicated me to the Lord as an infant,
and at 54 years of age laid her hands upon my head
to bless me
and the work God has called me to do.

To my mother-in-law, Wanda, my daughter, Jennifer,
and my daughters-in-law: Kelly, Elizabeth and Justin's wife,
whoever you are.

To my granddaughters, Mila, Zoe and Zayanna,
and to the future wives of my precious grandsons,
Zachary, Ezekiel and Zion.

To all my spiritual daughters, as well as every woman
in the earth.

May you all become women of power
who seize your destinies in Christ.

CONTENTS

7

Foreword

WHEN THERE IS an intercessory burden in your heart, you may be ambushed by God to be the very answer to your own prayers! Shirley Sustar was crying out for a spiritual mother/mentor and the wisdom she has gained over the years are now being written in book form to mentor not just one, but many who read *Become a Woman of Power*!

There are many fathers in the church who are raising up sons but very few mothers who are raising up daughters. I have a burning passion for the body of Christ to see fathers and mothers raising up sons and daughters in this next generation so we have a healthy family in the body of Christ. My heart's cry is to raise up double portion sons and daughters who will move in the Presence and power of the Spirit to become world changers! I want to pass a baton to them that is dripping with oil and the glory of His presence, not just some old dried up stick!

Become a Woman of Power is a trumpet call to activate and mentor women and challenge them to a deeper passion, greater power and significant purpose to advance the kingdom of God! Shirley identifies the fears women face and the vicious cycles and roadblocks the enemy uses against women to keep them hidden, paralyzed, spiritually barren and heart sick from hope that has been deferred.

Her book is replete with keys that bring revelation to unlock women's hearts and destinies. She is practical, humorous, and transparent as she beautifully illustrates the lessons the Lord has taught her. Shirley isn't just writing about mentoring, this is her lifestyle so she can give language and understanding to a subject that is rarely preached about, let alone demonstrated in the body of Christ!

There is nothing like a mother's sensitive and discerning heart when it beats in sync with the heart of Jesus! A woman is also unique in that God has given her the power to reproduce (as in the natural, so in the Spirit). *Become a Woman of Power* is not a call to rebellion, but a call to courage. It takes great courage for women to overcome the obstacles that are in the mindsets of the body of Christ and the onslaughts of the enemy.

In her book, Shirley tells about the time we met in Ohio and I asked her two burning questions that changed her life. I am asking those same questions to both the fathers and the mothers in the body of Christ! First of all, are you willing to be a forerunner and take a stand for women in ministry? The blessing of the Lord is on those who will stand with women in these final days! Secondly, are you willing to pay the price? Yes, there is a price to pay, but there is a greater price to pay for saying no. What will you say? What will you do?

Jill Austin
Author and conference speaker
Founder & President
Master Potter Ministries
Hollywood, California
www.masterpotter.com

Acknowledgments

FIRST AND FOREMOST I want to acknowledge my Lord and Savior, Jesus Christ, who found me, called me, chose me and continues to save me. Because You continually lead me in Your ways, I cannot help but seize my destiny. Thank You!

Secondly, my husband, pastor and best friend, Jim: You have kept your hand in my back while nudging me forward. You have repeatedly told me I can do all things through Christ who is my strength. Over twenty years ago you prophesied over my life, washed my feet and told me you would lay down your life to see me successful in God. You have been faithful to do that ever since. You are the greatest man of God I know and the wind beneath my wings. Thank you!

To my father, Don Lacas, and my father-in-law, the Rev. James Sustar: You have both told me I could do anything I set my mind to do. To Jim Goll, Lattie McDonough, Bill Beery, Denny Crammer, Ron King and all leading men in the Body of Christ who have helped prepare the way for God's daughters to come forth in His purposes: Your encouragement, wisdom and authority are helping to restore the Church to God's original purpose and power. And to every woman who has been a forerunner for women in ministry: You have paid a price that has cost you dearly. Thank you!

To my daughter and son-in-law, Jennifer and Japhet Ntia: You told me to write the book, and you continually intercede for me. To my sons and daughters-in-law, Jim, Kelly, Nathan and Elizabeth, and to my youngest son, Justin: You all have cheered me on. Thank you!

To Teri Beery, Jody Jarvis, Carol Mast, Jennifer Ntia, Karen Noe, Sheryl Villegas and Kathi Zickefoose: You were so kind to read the original rough draft and pray for its release. Thank you!

Finally, to Jane Campbell, Grace Sarber, Cheryl Van Andel, Sheila Ingram, Karen Steele, Stephanie Vink and the staff of Chosen/Baker Books: Thank you for your kindness and patience while I was learning along the way. I honor your excellent spirits and dedication to publish writing that edifies and builds up the Body of Christ. Thank you!

Introduction

On December 26, 1971, God's presence suddenly came into our living room and knocked my husband, Jim, to the floor! Not quite understanding what had just taken place, I positioned myself beside my husband, and together we wept bitter tears of repentance. Even though we both had been raised in Christian homes, the first five years of our marriage had been wasted in rebellion to God. In a quick moment that night, however, God powerfully and sovereignly apprehended us! He picked us up out of our sin and brokenness, gave us a revelation of His Lordship and thrust us into His purposes. Since that night over 33 years ago, we have not been the same. We are forever changed in devotion to God and His plan for our lives.

Eight years later during the Christmas school break of 1979, our young family eagerly anticipated our upcoming vacation to Southern California to visit relatives and friends. By this time Jim and I had three children ranging from four months to eight years of age. Since flying was not in our budget we decided to drive from Ohio, which also would allow for some quality family time. Because our children were small and accustomed to daily naps and early bedtimes, Jim made the backseat into a bed. During those hours when the children slept or quietly played, Jim and I talked. What some people might consider traveling the hard way was pure luxury for us. For more than a few days we were able to share our hearts with one another without work, doorbell or telephone interruptions.

Just before we left for our trip God had begun to speak to Jim's heart about the calling and ministry of a "father" in the Kingdom of God. At first it was God's still, small voice that Jim heard. Then words supporting these thoughts started coming from others, confirming this call. So while we traveled, the topic of fathering took up most of our conversation. We were not quite sure what God was requiring of Jim or how he would move toward this call. Our curiosity and love for God, however, stimulated much thought, discussion and anticipation. I realize now that the Lord was gently nudging my husband and depositing portions of His Father's heart into him. This ministry of a "father" has directed Jim's life ever since, and the fruit I have witnessed in my husband has been an expansion of love for mankind.

The ministry of a "father" is very biblical. The apostle Paul was a father to various believers and churches. He carried these saints in his heart and never ceased to pray for them. Even while he was in prison for preaching the Gospel, Paul communicated to them faithfully through letters. Through his writings Paul taught, nurtured and encouraged these believers in the ways of the Lord, exhorting them to grow in the wisdom and knowledge of Christ.

In his letter to the church at Ephesus, Paul asked the Ephesians not to lose heart—not to faint or become despondent through fear—at what he was suffering on their behalf. Rather, he told them to glory in it. Because of their love and high esteem for Paul, his suffering helped establish them in unity, prayer, evangelism and steadfast service to God. Paul told them that his suffering was actually an honor to them! The Father's heart that Paul had for the Ephesians caused him to rejoice even over his own suffering because it meant development and growth for the saints. Paul said, "For this reason [seeing the greatness of this plan by which you are built together in Christ], I bow my knees before the Father of our Lord Jesus Christ, For Whom every family in heaven and on earth is named [that Father from Whom all fatherhood takes its title and derives its name]" (Ephesians 3:14–15).

Fatherhood is a precious word to Jim and me, for it involves relationship. Fatherhood in the Kingdom requires God's love to expand within us and to reproduce itself in others. The word *fatherhood* within the Church is much more than a one-time evangelistic encounter; rather, it is a lifetime of knowing and loving others intimately. It also suggests overseeing and watching out for the welfare of souls.

I think the saddest thing that David, the psalmist, ever said was, "No man cared for my soul" (Psalm 142:4, KJV). The Amplified Bible says, "No man cares for my life or my welfare." Jesus taught that the first and foremost commandment is to love God with all one's heart, soul and mind. And the second is like it: "You shall love your neighbor as [you do] yourself" (Matthew 22:37–39). God's intention has always been that we watch out for the welfare of others. His commandment actually requires our love to expand until our concern for others is truly no different than our concern for ourselves. This second commandment encompasses the heart of our Father God, who loves us beyond measure and watches over us without ceasing, and who desires that we learn to love others as He loves them. He wants us to have His Father's heart for His people. As His love in us expands, we are better able to enter into the kind of intimate love for others that He desires.

The Body of Christ has not yet fully observed and followed these two commandments. We can be sure, however, that the world is watching, and this is no light thing! Jesus said the world would believe and be convinced that the Father sent the Son when they observe our love for one another (see John 17:21).

At this point you may be wondering, *Is this the right book?* I thought this was a book about *women* of power, not *men*, and especially not fathers. It is important for you to understand that it was my husband's call to operate more in the power of God that led to my own. With this new call of fatherhood upon Jim's life and my determination to be a good wife, I became his greatest cheerleader. I repeatedly encouraged him to heed the word of the Lord, whatever that might mean. Little did I realize by agreeing with my husband at that time what I soon would discover about my own role as a "mother" in God's Kingdom!

Shortly after this, during our trip to California, God began to reveal His plan for me. He began to show me that He was creating in me a mother's heart that would enable me to better share His love with others—and in so doing, He was giving me an opportunity to share in the call He had placed upon my husband with a similar call of my own.

God's transforming process in our hearts and lives always comes first by revelation, then by acting upon our responsibility to that revelation, and finally our lives produce a message out of that revelation. The revelation in Jim's life and his decision to act upon it, coupled with my support of God's call on His life, has led to a revelation of my own and a life message that we now share and teach to others.

As you read *Become a Woman of Power*, my prayer is that you will begin to experience God's will for you and your ministry as a mother in His Kingdom. I pray you will be challenged to give yourself to maturity and training. I pray your heart will be stirred and stretched beyond its comfort zone. I pray it will expand and leap into the hearts and needs of others, ministering God's love and purposes to them—just as the Lord continues to stir, stretch and expand my own heart to do. I am praying that every young Christian woman will submit her life to the development and training for ministry. I am praying for every older, godly woman to be motivated, activated and released to give away what she already has.

The days of comfortably serving ourselves as we play church are over. May we all recognize the urgency of the hour and get ready for the great, mighty and soon-coming harvest!

1

CALLED TO BE A MOTHER
IN THE KINGDOM

I N THE INTRODUCTION I shared with you how setting off on that trip to California in 1979 was the beginning of God's revealing His purpose for my ministry, but I would like to tell you the rest of the story. After arriving in California and celebrating Christmas with my family members, we packed our suitcases again and went to spend the remaining part of our vacation with our dear friends Jim and Carol Hilbrant. We had met the Hilbrants at church eight years earlier in 1971 when they were newlyweds, and by the time they had Laura, their first child, we had become more like family than mere friends. Together we shared many memories.

Just before Jim and I had moved from California, both our families also went through a difficult and painful trial involving the church where we had been members. So our memories included not only good times, but also times of tears. With every trial and disappointment we face, the enemy tries to wound and destroy us. Yet God uses difficult situations to develop spiritual growth in our lives. We understood that the trying of our faith always strengthens and perfects us, so we looked forward to sharing with the Hilbrants what God had been doing in all our lives.

Being together with the Hilbrants was a joyful time. The first few days with Jim and Carol were spent talking and laughing until our faces hurt. We talked about the cities in which we lived and the churches where God had placed us. Jim and Carol highly esteemed their new pastors, Dave and Vivian Cunningham, and we eagerly looked forward to meeting them at a luncheon planned for later that week.

On the day of the luncheon, Carol awoke feeling ill. She insisted on joining us, though, and while the two families scurried to get ready, I stopped thinking about Carol's condition—until our luncheon.

After we had been introduced and cordially greeted by the Cunninghams, Vivian turned toward Carol and asked if she was feeling all right. Carol tried to assure her that she was okay, but Vivian proceeded to examine Carol for herself. Placing her hand upon Carol's forehead, Vivian checked for a fever, while fussing that Carol was not dressed warmly enough.

At that moment I began to feel irritated, and almost everything Vivian did after that annoyed me. Yet Vivian did not do anything wrong. Instead, she was warm, kind, gracious and loving to everyone.

I realized I was feeling this way because of the attention Vivian was giving to Carol. I envied their friendship and did not want this new person to be so attentive to my friend. I also knew my feelings were ridiculous. I tried to ignore them and silently told myself to knock it off! I never justified—at any moment—the attitude of my heart. In fact, I spent the majority of the time silently repenting and asking God to tell me what my problem was. I was truly convicted and grieved by the way my heart responded in jealousy, and I understood what God's Word says concerning it. It is a terrible thing—"like rottenness of the bones" (Proverbs 14:30)!

God knows I did not like myself just then. But when Vivian asked Carol for the third time if she was warm enough, I heard my mouth exclaim, "If you are not warm enough, Carol, I am sure Vivian would be happy to loan you her sweater."

I could not believe my own ears, to say nothing of my catty mouth. I am usually not a rude person. In fact, I hate rudeness more than almost anything. Even though I had spoken those words with a deceitful smile and even though no one seemed to notice my attitude, I knew I had been out of line and my attitude stunk. While my face was turning red, Vivian heaped hot coals upon my head by pointing to her sweater and softly saying, "Of course!"

The only thing I could think to do at that moment was to excuse myself to go to the restroom. I wanted to cry! I wanted to run! Inside my head I was screaming questions at God: "What is the matter with me? I have never felt like this before!"

To make matters worse, as I attempted to remove myself from my chair, I and everyone else at our table discovered I had been sitting the entire time with my wrap skirt caught up over the back of it. For the life of me, I do not know how this happened. As I struggled to become untangled from my chair, the confusion made me think I had been revealing my undergarment while I sat. I guess the look on my face was hilarious!

The group instantaneously exploded into laughter while I fought to free myself. Poor Jim just sat there shaking his head, saying in a tone of wonder, "Only you. These things only happen to you!" Being humbled and having to laugh at myself somewhat lifted my unreasonable and curious irritation and to a point changed the atmosphere surrounding my heart.

But God, I Did Not Mean to Expose Myself!

Vivian's freedom to love in a tangible way confronted my limitations to love one of my dearest and closest friends. That afternoon, however, God began revealing to me the attitudes, fears and insecurities hidden in my heart. My flesh struggled against seeing the ugliness of my heart, and as I struggled to maintain my composure I ended up exposing my "self"! Even though laughter helped brighten the moment for me, my chief concern suddenly was turned toward a more serious exposure than my slip. I had not understood why I struggled so during our meeting until later, when I realized God had been speaking to my heart through Vivian's actions.

"For the Lord sees not as man sees; for man looks on the outward appearance, but the Lord looks on the heart" (1 Samuel 16:7). When God reveals and exposes our hearts before our eyes, His intention is for us to see the revealed sins and weaknesses as a roadblock to a great destiny. Wrong attitudes and sinful ways tolerated in our lives not only keep us from achieving greatness for His name's sake but also blind and bind our insight from seeing into His ways and purposes—and even the very call, purpose and desire of our own hearts. When this happens, we prevent ourselves from growing and developing into the potential and purpose for which we were created.

A Mother's Heart

After leaving the restaurant we all said good-bye to Dave and Vivian, and Jim and I climbed into the backseat of the Hilbrants' car. Immediately I began to dread the questions Jim and Carol might ask about the time we had spent with their new pastors. Because my attitude had been so terribly self-centered, I am afraid I really had not listened or joined into much of the conversation. I had not given much thought to the Cunninghams, other than their obvious love for our friends and the fact that when we returned home to Ohio we would not be able to practically experience the relationship with the Hilbrants we held so dear.

I was sure the two Jims would have a lot to say about the similar vision we all held. Because of my attitude, I decided it would be best if I sat silently while they talked. I was certain that if I just smiled a lot and quietly nodded in agreement, I would eventually get rid of the ugly feeling in my gut.

"So, Shirley, what did you think of Vivian?" our friend Jim asked pointedly.

In somewhat of a panic, I searched quickly through my ugly jealousy to the truths I had beheld. In my silent thoughts I realized I truly did admire Vivian's heart of love and her freedom to express her love with words and touch. I found myself saying, "I really admire her mother's heart."

Jim Hilbrant immediately responded by saying, "Oh, yes, she has a wonderful mother's heart—but you know, Shirley, I see that same heart in you!"

I looked up at my husband with somewhat of a shocked look, and he quietly responded, "Did you think God would call me to be a father and not call you to be a mother?"

Because Jim and Carol were in the front seat with their backs toward us, they could not see the tears running down my face. I know the three of them continued their conversation about our time in the restaurant, but I could not tell you what was said. I was completely lost in conversation with God.

In my mind, I began to see pictures of different women God had brought into my life through the years. God had given me favor with these women, and often I would share with them the things I learned from the Lord. These women were my friends, and I cherished each one of them deeply. The fact that we all held the same hunger for God added to our closeness. I loved to see them excel in God and would rejoice with them over God's blessings in their lives.

I realized that, like Vivian, I would often feel an impulse to help button a coat, pick lint off their clothing as we spoke or even touch a forehead if one of these dear friends was not feeling well. I, too, desired to fuss over women whom the Father brought into my life. But instead of doing these things I would hold myself back from what I thought might be imposing myself upon them. As these different friends came to my mind, I responded to the thought of mothering them by telling the Lord I did not think I was more mature than they were.

The Lord immediately answered my confusion by saying, *I want you to imagine two women. One woman is eighty and the other woman is sixty years old. Tell me, which one is more mature?*

I knew God was not referring to age, so I responded by saying, "Neither, Lord. Both are fully mature women."

Yes, the Lord answered, *but the eighty-year-old is the mother of the sixty-year-old. It does not matter how old her daughter becomes, the mother will never stop concerning herself with her daughter's welfare. She will rejoice when she rejoices and weep when she weeps. She will wonder if her daughter is eating right and will continually pray for her welfare. She would rather suffer than have her daughter lack anything. When her daughter succeeds, her mother's heart will beam, and when she fails, she will graciously cover her with encouragement and hope. Age has nothing to do with their relationship. She is simply her mother!*

Then the Lord said, *I am not speaking to you about maturity at this time, but about the burden in your heart, for I have called you to be a mother in My Kingdom.*

Suddenly I realized God had been speaking to my heart through Vivian's actions. I just had not been listening. My primary focus had been on myself and my feelings while my mind was anxiously sweating over things I did not understand. God gave me a little seminar that day on mothers in the Kingdom: Vivian was my seminar from God.

God Continues His Work in Us

God is working in our lives, and He will work everything together for good to those who love Him and are called according to His purposes (see Romans 8:28). Philippians 1:6 says, "And I am convinced and sure of this very thing, that He who began a good work in you will continue until the day of Jesus Christ—right up to the time of His return—developing [that good work] and perfecting and bringing it to full completion in you."

Spending that afternoon with Vivian caused me to understand more clearly an aspect of the good work God has called me to do. Through meeting with Vivian God was able to plant a desire in my heart for freedom of fear and insecurities pertaining to relationships. That day I began to understand that God wants to express His tangible love to others through His family and would do so through me as I embraced a mother's heart.

When I realized God had just shown me a living demonstration of what He was calling and working in me to become, I was determined to step beyond my comfort zone. After I returned home from our trip to California, my friends recognized my newfound freedom. They said something was different about me even before I had a chance to share with them what had happened.

When we allow God to do a work in our lives, He transforms us! Even though it would be nineteen years before I would see Vivian again, God used her in that one encounter to dramatically change my heart and thinking. In both practical and spiritual behavior Vivian was a model of peace and security that enabled her to naturally love, care and watch over others—with supernatural results! Her life motivated me toward maturity.

I am grateful for and will never forget her example as a mother in the Kingdom. Because of it I was able to recognize my need for growth so that one day I might also fulfill my God-given mandate.

God's People Are Crying Out for Mothers

For thirty-some years now, the heart of a mother has been developing within me and I have been learning what it means to be a mother in God's Kingdom. I have learned that a good mother is not one who is perfect but one who is willing to be perfected! I am learning through God's Word, through natural and practical parenting with my own children, through my relationships within the Church and through my many mistakes. The Lord has dealt with me to always remember where I have come from and what I have been through in my walk with Him.

With each lesson and new understanding I have become more confident of one thing: In all God calls us to do and accomplish, our mandate is to walk with Him and to love others in the same manner He loves us. Love is what makes us effective.

Today the hearts of God's people are crying out for mothers in the Kingdom to arise in their midst. Just as fathers are coming forth in this hour to instruct, mentor and train those who will follow the path of our mighty King, God also is releasing mothers to mentor, instruct, train and comfort His people.

2

WHERE IS MY MOTHER?

I ABSOLUTELY LOVE CARING for my husband, my family and my home. It is part of who I am and part of what fulfills me. There have been occasions in that area of love and service, however, when I have protested candidly that I am not everyone's slave! Just as it is in the natural realm, the flip side of the very thing that delights and fulfills our hearts can grow sour if we feel taken for granted in areas of ministry.

Shortly after understanding God's call to mentor women, I went through a season of feeling very used and unappreciated. One particular evening when I was exhausted and had decided to go to bed early, the phone rang. My husband was on the line for just a few moments. After hanging up, he announced that a couple from church was on their way over to visit and would arrive in about twenty minutes.

I told him I wished he had checked with me first because I really did not want company. I did not feel well and had wanted to go to bed. Jim proceeded to encourage me to put a smile on my face and to fix myself up a bit. He told me that while I was doing that, he would prepare something to serve them. He mentioned how excited the woman was to see me and said, "Shirley, she really loves you!"

Like an erupting volcano, I snapped, "Nobody loves me—they only neeeed me!" Then I cried out sarcastically, "I feel like everybody's mother! Where is *my* mother?"

I could tell by his dropped jaw and bulging eyes that Jim was shocked by my sudden outburst. But I did not care. I demanded that he tell me how I could go on without a mother to mentor me. I have no explanation for the way I behaved other than hormones, and I now refer to that moment as a hormonal fit.

For the sake of Christian decency, I did get my act together before our friends arrived. Yet that night it was as if a wound had afflicted my soul and my heart became dissatisfied by the absence of a mentor to train me. My own mother lived three thousand miles away, and it seemed there was no one who had gone before me who was willing to invest in my life. My heart began crying for a spiritual mother from whom I could learn, someone who would bring me to maturity by her example, instructions, counsel and correction.

Searching for an Answer

A few weeks later, Jim and I attended a conference for pastors and their wives in Washington, D.C. After one of the workshops I approached the speaker to ask for counsel concerning this cry of my heart. I immediately realized, however, that we were on two different tracks of thinking when she said, "If you want friends, you must show yourself friendly." She spent the next few minutes trying to encourage me in creative ways to win friends and establish close relationships with other women.

I decided against telling her I had more relationships than I wanted at the moment, that what I needed and was craving was a mentor. In that instant I realized there was no immediate answer. All the talking and crying in the world would not meet my need. I would simply have to pray and wait on God.

Ready in Season

During the main conference session that afternoon God averted my attention to a young woman sitting about three rows in front of me. She was weeping in her seat while the rest of us stood in worship. I could tell that her weeping had nothing to do with worship but was coming from a broken heart. Immediately the Lord spoke to me and said, *Go ask her if she would like to step into the lobby to talk and pray with you.*

In obedience, I went to her at once. Her reply, however, was, "No, thank you! If you feel like praying for me, go ahead and pray as you feel led."

I said a quick little prayer and then returned to my seat. But a few moments later, the Lord told me to go to her again. I wrestled with His word to me for a while but finally approached her a second time. I told her that even though I did not know what was troubling her, God had put her burden upon me and I truly desired to help her in some way. Again I made myself available to talk and pray with her, but the woman's response was exactly the same as before.

As I turned to go back, I felt very foolish. All eyes seemed to be upon me. I thought I must have appeared intrusive and overbearing to everyone around me, and to top it off I was prob-ably embarrassing my husband! Yet when I returned to my seat, the Lord said, *Go back again.*

While I was wrestling with my own quiet rebellion God said, *This time tell her you have been married for nineteen years.*

Whenever God tells me to do something I am uncomfortable with or that requires stretching on my part, I give myself a pep talk. "I can do this!" I tell myself. "So what if I look like a fool? I will never see these people again."

God has a sense of humor, however, and I often hear, *Yes, you will—you are going to spend eternity with them.*

I approached the woman, apologizing, "I am soooo sorry! I really don't want to impose myself upon you, but . . . I've been married for nineteen years."

Suddenly she stood up, grabbed her Bible and purse and said, "Let's go!"

I thought, "God, You could have told me that the first time."

As we sat together in the lobby, this woman poured out her heart to me. She had been married for nine years and was a frustrated pastor's wife. For years she had been trying to work through the adjustments of balancing the family she loved and a church that required most of her husband's time and atten-tion. The women of her church were looking to her for counsel and instruction, but she felt inadequate and lonely. Because of all these things, bitterness had settled in her heart. Sobbing overcame her words as she then told me that both her mother and grandmother had passed away recently.

I took her hand and said, "And you need a mother." She inter-rupted me before I finished my sentence and answered, "Yes! I need a mother."

I reminded her that Psalm 68:6 says, "God places the solitary in families and gives the desolate a home in which to dwell." He is a family Man! From the beginning of time, God established families that produced tribes and tribes that produced nations. In the family of God are mothers, fathers, sisters and brothers to love and help care for one another as members of one household. Romans 12:10 says, "Love one another with brotherly affection [as members of one family], giving precedence and showing honor to one another." God's intention is for His purposes to be accomplished by one family, the people of God.

I looked into the woman's eyes and said, "I am not really smart, but I am certain of this: God has given me a mother's heart. I may never see you again, but today God has placed us together so that I might help meet a need you have."

For the next hour and a half the woman shared her heart with me, and during that time I was able to encourage and counsel her. I watched her countenance change before my eyes as a spirit of heaviness lifted and peace and joy were restored to her.

Sometimes we just need to be able to talk, to have someone really listen to our hearts and to hear the words, "I have been there. You are going to make it!" As we were saying good-bye, I encouraged the woman to pray that God would raise up someone to be a mother to her, just as I had been praying that very thing for myself. As I was speaking, the Lord instructed me to tell her, "In the meantime, look into God's Word. In it He has placed women who will teach, train and mentor you according to His purpose for your life."

We hugged one another, and I stood and watched her as she walked away. I was amazed at what had just transpired. As I thought about the words God had just spoken to her, the Lord spoke to me and said, *Yes, remember that! At the time of your cry you did not really need a mother. You just wanted a pity party. When you need one, I will raise one up just as I did for her. In the meantime, however, look into My Word. In it are women who will teach, train and mentor you according to My purpose for your life.* My perpetual wound was instantly healed, and from that time I have had no occasion to whine for a mother!

And since that conference in Washington, D.C., over eighteen years ago, God has given me older women in the faith to mentor me in different areas of ministry. I know these women are for me, and I know they love me. They have encouraged me by saying things like, "If I can do it, Shirley, then you can do it!" They have corrected me. They have blessed and comforted me through precious words such as, "I am proud of you!"

Mothers in the Word

Just as God had directed me to do, I began digging into the Bible to read about the adventures and exploits of different women. These women have helped motivate, train and encourage me. They have challenged, corrected and stirred me toward godliness. Their examples have literally cheered me on.

> And all of these, though they won divine approval by [means of] their faith, did not receive the fulfillment of what was promised, Because God had us in mind and had something better and greater in view for us, so that they [these heroes and heroines of faith] should not come to perfection apart from us [before we could join them]. Therefore then, since we are surrounded by so great a cloud of witnesses [who have borne testimony to the Truth], let us strip off and throw aside every encumbrance (unnecessary weight) and that sin which so readily (deftly and cleverly) clings to and entangles us, and let us run with patient

endurance and steady and active persistence the appointed course of the race that is set before us.

Hebrews 11:39–40; 12:1

Hebrews 11 also lists the heroes—and heroines—of the Christian faith. Among these, and one of only two women mentioned, is Abraham's wife, Sarah.

Sarah: A Mother in the Kingdom

In the Middle East during biblical times it was a reproach for a woman to be childless. God had promised Sarah many children, but her body had remained unproductive. In addition, she was far past the age of childbearing. It seemed it was too late for her body to fulfill God's personal word to her. Through the years, Sarah chose to follow her husband and the word God had spoken pertaining to their destinies. Because she chose to trust God, she was not afraid of submission. She understood that God would be faithful to watch over and protect His word concerning their lives. She put her trust in Him. She chose to embrace a meek and quiet spirit. Because of this, God changed her name from *Sarai*, meaning "dominant," to *Sarah*, which means "princess." "And God said to Abraham, As for Sarai your wife, you shall not call her name Sarai, but Sarah [Princess] her name shall be. And I will bless her and give you a son also by her. Yes, I will bless her, and she shall be a mother of nations; kings of peoples shall come from her" (Genesis 17:15–16). And Sarah had faith to believe that God would perform His will through them.

Of course, we all know that Sarah was not perfect! She made some wrong choices and sometimes tried to accomplish God's will through her own efforts. Sarah chose, however, to learn from her mistakes. God looked at her heart, and because of her humility and grace He not only changed her name but also changed the circumstances of her life. He miraculously changed Sarah's life from barrenness and disgrace to fruitfulness and honor, making her a mother of nations with kings of peoples coming from her.

Sarah was one of the first mothers in God's Kingdom. The story of her life is one biblical example God used to teach me about His will for my life ministry. The apostle Peter said we are true daughters of Sarah if we do right, let nothing terrify us, do not give way to hysterical fears and do not let anxieties unnerve us (see 1 Peter 3:6). God wants His daughters to walk in humility and grace and to let their hearts trust in Him.

As you can see from my "Vivian Seminar" that I told you about in chapter 1, my first reaction to something I do not understand is often irritation! When my mind does not understand or my flesh wants to reject what God is trying to reveal to my spirit, my soul experiences temporary turmoil. Like sandpaper softens and changes rough wood by friction against its grain, in like manner God brings paradigm shifts and clarity to my understanding. His ways and purposes often cause friction against the grain of my human wisdom before I am softened and changed toward His will. I may be slow, but for me God's wisdom and understanding do not come overnight. They are things I must receive and choose to get!

"The beginning of Wisdom is: get Wisdom (skillful and godly Wisdom)! [For skillful and godly Wisdom is the principal thing.] And with all you have gotten, get understanding (discernment, comprehension, and interpretation)" (Proverbs 4:7). Truly, when we "get understanding," we will have gained a full definition and explanation of what we were seeking to know. We will have achieved good sense, judgment, distinction and sharpness because we will have grasped and attained it for ourselves!

God is not in a hurry. He will not give up on us or the plan He has for our lives. While I am getting understanding, it is best to be still so I can remember and know that He is in control. If we embrace a meek and quiet spirit while we wait on Him, like Sarah did, then revelation will come. Revelation does not come easily, however, if one's spirit is loud and anxious.

A loud and anxious spirit has nothing to do with the volume of one's voice or how much he or she talks. It has everything to do with fear, impatience and a jealous or striving heart. A meek and quiet spirit, on the other hand, has everything to do with humility and grace. First Peter 3:4 says a humble spirit is very precious in God's sight, and two verses later Sarah is again held up as an example for us (see verse 6).

God has taught me how vital it is that women in His Kingdom strive for a meek, teachable and humble spirit. When we humble ourselves and trust God to work in and through our lives, He releases understanding to our hearts so we can walk out His purposes.

Ruth and Naomi

Ruth and Naomi are two biblical heroines whose lives also have ministered to me. Their godly mother/daughter mentoring relationship is a wonderful example.

The book of Ruth tells us that a famine occurred in the days when the judges ruled Israel. Because of this, Elimelech, an Israelite from Bethlehem of Judah, traveled to the country of Moab with his wife, Naomi, and their two sons, Mahlon and Chilion, to make a new home. After Elimelech died, their two sons married Moabite women, Orpah and Ruth. Ten years later, however, both Mahlon and Chilion also died, leaving their mother and wives suddenly without care and support.

Naomi heard how the Lord had visited His people Israel and had given them food, so she decided to pack up her belongings and return to her relatives in Bethlehem. As the two daughters-in-law began to set out with her, she stopped them and said, "Go, return each of you to her mother's house. May the Lord deal kindly with you, as you have dealt with the dead and with me. The Lord grant that you may find a home and rest, each in the house of her husband! Then she kissed them and they wept aloud" (Ruth 1:8–9).

Orpah wept while she kissed her mother-in-law good-bye, and then she turned to go back to her own people. She probably hoped to remarry and stay in familiarity until she died. Ruth also wept. Her tears, however, were of another nature. They were not because she was going to miss Naomi, but because she could not bear the thought of being separated from her. Ruth's heart was so interwoven with Naomi's, so committed to the relationship God had given them, that she would not and could not go! Her response was a lifetime covenant:

> Urge me not to leave you or to turn back from following you; for where you go I will go, and where you lodge I will lodge. Your people shall be my people and your God my God. Where you die I will die, and there will I be buried. The Lord do so to me, and more also, if anything but death parts me from you.
>
> Ruth 1:16–17

Ruth had been born and raised in Moab. But when she married her husband, she chose to lose her life and identity in him, making his life hers! Because she chose to lose her life, she found it in the only true and wise God.

> He who loves [and takes more pleasure in] father or mother more than [in] Me is not worthy of Me; and he who loves [and takes more pleasure in] son or daughter more than [in] Me is not worthy of Me; And he who does not take up his cross and follow Me [cleave steadfastly to Me, conforming wholly to My example in living and, if need be, in dying also] is not worthy of Me. Whoever finds his [lower] life will lose it [the higher life], and whoever loses his [lower] life on My account will find it [the higher life].
>
> Matthew 10:37–39

Ruth believed in God and made the decision to follow Him. Realizing her need to learn a new and living way to walk, she looked to Naomi to teach and mentor her in the ways of God. Naomi was the epitome of godliness in both character and behavior. She not only knew God's holy laws, but she also understood His principles for living. Throughout the book of Ruth, Naomi called Ruth her daughter. Even though Ruth was really her daughter-in-law, their love for one another was as intimate as if Ruth were her own.

A Committed Relationship Bears Fruit

Ruth 1:19–21 says that when Naomi went home to her people, the whole town was stirred about their arrival, asking, "Is this Naomi?" Naomi told her friends and relatives not to call

her *Naomi* because it meant "pleasant," but to call her *Mara*, or
"bitter." At that point in her life, she truly believed the Almighty
had dealt her a bitter hand. She said she had gone out of Bethlehem full, but God had afflicted her and returned her home
empty! By staying with Naomi in her most distraught time,
Ruth showed honor to her mother-in-law, faithfully staying
with her and working to provide for her. She was even willing
to grovel in poverty, knowing God would make a way for them
somehow. Ruth would not allow Naomi to give up. Ruth's commitment to her mentor and the Truth her mentor had taught
overpowered Naomi's present bitterness. Because of Ruth's patience and love, Naomi once again was able to see the hand of
God move in her life.

The respect and affection Ruth had for Naomi was so evident and obvious that reports of how she treated her mother-
in-law reached Naomi's kinsman, Boaz, who was a good man
and very wealthy. When Naomi realized God had given Ruth
favor with Boaz, she instructed Ruth step by step in ways to
cultivate a relationship with him. Ruth had not been familiar
with the conduct and ways of the people in this new kingdom,
but because she listened and received instruction and wisdom
from her mentor, she accomplished the purpose and plan God
had for her life: Ruth eventually became Boaz's wife. Later when
Ruth conceived a son, she insisted that Naomi remain with her
to help teach and instruct him. Thus, God provided for both
Ruth and Naomi in every way.

The joy and celebration of Ruth and Boaz's new child ex-
tended throughout their neighborhood. The neighbor women
all gathered around Naomi and said, "Blessed be the Lord, Who
has not left you this day without a close kinsman, and may his
name be famous in Israel. And may he be to you a restorer of

life and a nourisher and supporter in your old age, for your daughter-in-law who loves you, who is better to you than seven sons, has borne him" (Ruth 4:14–15). Then Naomi took the child in her arms and became his nurse. The neighbor women gave him the name Obed, and he became the father of Jesse, the father of King David, an ancestor of Jesus Christ! So not only did God provide for the two women, but He also blessed them beyond measure!

Ruth was a woman of loyalty who committed herself to God and His people. She was wisely devoted to training for the Kingdom. I do not believe Ruth ever imagined such greatness and honor. How could she know what God would do for her or through her? She had decided to follow God because she believed in Him and loved Him. Because of her love, she desired to learn of Him. Ruth put her trust and hope in God and continually submitted to the mentor who had gone before her.

Ruth deeply loved and appreciated Naomi, her mentor. She never forgot that Naomi had brought her into God's family and taught her His ways. Even though she had once been an outsider, a Moabite, God grafted her into His Kingdom, and from her life eternal, royal descendants were produced!

God Will Answer Your Cry

The stories of Sarah, Ruth and Naomi are wonderful starting places for women who want to learn more from the mentors God gave us in His Word. If we let Him, He will pour out revelation and understanding to us through mentors like these and others He holds up as examples for us. With some, we can consider and elaborate on their lives in great measure because of the length and detail that is given. Others are just barely mentioned. Yet from them all we are able to draw strength and encouragement to fulfill our personal mandate from the Lord. We can be thankful for their examples and trust that even today they are cheering us on in righteous living.

God wants us to look to His Word for the fulfillment of all our needs. In it He has provided the answer to our every question. And in His time, God will raise up and establish mentors for our lives. We can trust His faithfulness to us!

My Own Mother

As a final note to this chapter, I want to add that God has recently opened my eyes to something I did not know before and has given me a precious new gift. Many years ago my own mother, Alice Lacas, heard the audible voice of God and had a vision of the Lord calling her to Africa. That call and purpose, however, was never developed because my father was not open to that call as a young man. Because of that, my mother never mentioned it again. After 62 years of marriage, the Lord suddenly called my father home. Though death separated them and sadness loomed in my mother's life, just as with Naomi joy awaited, for God did not leave her without a close Kinsman, our Lord Jesus, who is "a restorer of life and a nourisher and supporter in [her] old age" (Ruth 4:14–15).

Now at 85 years of age, my mother has entered into a new beginning of grace in her life. God's calling and anointing on her life had lain dormant for a time but are now awakening at His appointed time. She will not go physically to Africa, but God's burdens and calling to the nations have once again risen upon her heart and now, through spiritual insight and intercessory prayer, she has the ability to touch and affect the lives of many and to bring changes to that continent. Also, some of her great-grandchildren are of African descent. I believe her age, 85, is even significant. In biblical numerology, eight is the number of new beginnings and five is the number of grace. I believe, therefore, that God has chosen this time in her life to pour out His grace and to restore my mother to His purposes, giving her a new beginning in Him. Though she thought God could no longer use her, through Christ He is restoring her life and is nourishing and supporting her in her old age. The Lord truly has turned her "mourning into dancing" and has "put off [her] sackcloth and girded [her] with gladness" (Psalm 30:11).

My husband and I cherish her prayers and blessing. We anticipate her encouragement and counsel. I believe she will become one of my greatest cheerleaders! She is excited about the call of God on our lives, and because of who she is to me, her cheerleading encourages me the greatest. I am encouraged and greatly blessed when any seasoned man or woman of God tells me he or she is proud of me for enduring hardship to seize my destiny in Christ, but when my own mother recognizes the call of God on my life and says the same thing, it has a much greater impact on my heart. It involves healings and strength I did not even realize I needed.

How grateful I am for my mother!

3

Is There a Mother in the House?

It seems that everywhere I go and everywhere I turn, women are looking for role models who love God, their families, the Church and the world as Christ does. They are looking for women who have gone before them walking with Christ and have the wisdom to prove it! They are seeking guidance in relationships, instruction in character, training in behavior and counsel through difficulties. If they are married, they are looking for women who not only love and respect their husbands but also whose husbands are obviously head over heels in love with their wives. Younger women with children are looking for older women who have experienced both good times and hard times rearing their own and have survived!

Is there a mother in the house? is a cry being heralded throughout the heavenly realm. It is both a question and a call.

The Call of God to Mothers in the Kingdom

Every daughter born is a potential mother! When I gave birth to my only daughter, Jennifer, I began looking forward to the day that she, too, would give birth to her own children. At only three years of age, her father and I beheld her heart's desire to one day become a mother like me. It was fun to watch Jennifer play house as she tried to imitate everything she observed me doing.

By the time her younger brother, Jimmy, was in kindergarten, her role as "big sister" looked more like the role of "mother smother." Seven-year-old Jennifer concerned herself daily about his welfare and behavior. Poor Jimmy! He still teases her today about the way she would routinely pop into his classroom to ask his teacher how he was doing. Sometimes after she would ask whether or not he was behaving himself, she would address an embarrassed Jimmy from across the room and say, "Be a good boy now, and if you need anything, remember I am just down the hall." Even though countless degrees of maturity needed to develop within her, the heart of a mother was obvious even at the ripe old age of seven.

A few years ago I finally became a grandmother. Before my grandson's birth, I found myself diligently watching over Jennifer's welfare. I was happy to drop whatever I was doing to help meet a need she might have. I anticipated my daughter's delivery as if it were my own, and the closer we got to that time the more excited and intense I became.

I did not want to impose myself upon Jennifer or her husband, Japhet. They repeatedly told me, however, that they not only wanted me with them during the birth, but they also needed me there. The more Jennifer sought my wisdom and help, the more released I felt to impart to her whatever I could. As they pulled on my help, they pulled on my wisdom and activated me toward instruction and care.

During her time of labor, it was an honor to rub Jennifer's back while I encouraged her through some rough times. After every contraction peaked, I would remind her of her coming reward. What a privilege it was to help my daughter give birth! Her God-given mother's heart was finally fulfilled with her very own gift from God! And my heart was blessed beyond measure as I worked to help my daughter give birth to what God had for her.

Just as God designed women physically to give birth and raise children, every daughter in the Kingdom is designed to reproduce spiritual life. And the clear purpose and role of mentors is to patiently work to help His daughters give birth to what God has for them.

God is raising up more than midwives to help birth His purposes. He is establishing women with mothers' hearts to help His people. A mother has an invested interest in the lives of her children. It is an interest that has been wrought by love. A mother's influence goes beyond helping her daughters give birth. It continues through counsel, teaching and training them concerning their gifts, calling and future lives.

God is moving in the hearts of both the old and the young within the Body of Christ. The older women are beginning to arise as mothers in His Kingdom by giving place to their instincts to reproduce and nurture others in what God has deposited within them. Young women are recognizing their need to be mentored in the ways of Christ and are seeking out women who will encourage, challenge and train them to produce excellent fruit.

From one end of the earth to the other, the Father is calling His daughters to His purposes, and we women are responding to His call to be mothers and be mentored by mothers in the Kingdom. His desire and delight is for us to grow up for Christ's sake and for the sake of the Kingdom. God has chosen us and has planted us where we are in order for us to bear substantial, visible fruit that will last. Then whatever we ask in His name will be done because our very lives characterize His name (see John 15:16). If we are not bearing the fruit that Jesus said His Spirit would work to produce in us, then we have not yet come to maturity.

> But the fruit of the [Holy] Spirit [the work which His presence within accomplishes] is love, joy (gladness), peace, patience (an even temper, forbearance), kindness, goodness (benevolence), faithfulness, Gentleness,(meekness, humility) self-control (self-restraint, continence). Against such things there is no law [that can bring a charge]. And those who belong to Christ Jesus (the Messiah) have crucified the flesh (the godless human nature) with its passions and appetites and desires. If we live by the [Holy] Spirit, let us also walk by the Spirit. [If by the Holy Spirit we have our life in God, let us go forward walking in line, our conduct controlled by the Spirit.]
>
> Galatians 5:22–25

Will We Heed the Call?

I grew up in Southern California. Because of the excellent weather, I spent the majority of my time playing outdoors as a child. It did not matter what I was doing or how much fun

I was having: When I heard the call coming from one of my parents—"Shirrrrley!"—I had only one wise choice, and that was to answer the call. Whenever I heard the voice beckoning me, my immediate response was always to run toward it answering, "I'm coming!" If I did not heed the call and chose to ignore my responsibility to it, I would face the consequences. Not only would I miss what had been prepared for me in terms of a meal, but I would also suffer the pain of disobedience.

Today the voice of God is calling, *Is there a mother in the house?* Will you heed the call? Will you run toward it? Will you be responsible to the call? If you do not, then you are going to miss out on so much that the Father has in store for you, and you will have to face the consequences. All of the stretching and pulling taking place within our spirits has been for the development of maturity and for the preparation of motherhood. God has purposed that we carry deep within our spiritual wombs His passion for the salvation of souls until the time we give birth through intercession. God's timing is perfect. Let's not miss the privilege and high purpose of His call.

It is also important to recognize that the devil opposes and tries to frustrate God's call by whispering vain imaginations in our ears; that is, he tries to persuade us that God's will and purpose for our lives is just our imagination speaking and we are thinking too highly of ourselves. This often causes a temporary setback for those who are humble or broken. If his attempts do not stop our pursuit to seize God's call for our lives, then Satan attempts to disqualify us. If he can get us to illegitimately position ourselves in what God is still developing within us, then the work of our hands will not be an acceptable offering but rather a blemished and rejected offering because our own pride has tried to establish it. "For God sets Himself against the proud (the insolent, the overbearing, the disdainful, the presumptuous, the boastful)—[and He opposes, frustrates and defeats them], but gives grace (favor, blessing) to the humble" (1 Peter 5:5).

If we will allow the humbling process of maturity to take place within our lives, then God will establish and bless the very work of our hands. Then the fruit coming from our lives will line up with the characteristics of Christ. If not, we will embarrass ourselves and others in the process, and we will not be able to fulfill His call.

It Is Also a Question God's Daughters Must Answer

Is there a mother in the house? It is not only a call. The Father is also asking a question. To understand the weighty seriousness of this question, let's compare it with the question *Is there a doctor in the house?* When the latter call is given, there is no doubt of a serious and immediate need! In the same way, the need for mothers in the Kingdom is a very serious and immediate need and one that is very important to our Lord.

Why? Imagine gazing upon a hard, frozen field in the middle of winter. As far as the eyes can see in every direction—north, south, east and west—there is only this frozen field. The owner, however, knows it will not be long before the ground will thaw and new life will spring up everywhere. Though others may drive by this field every day without taking notice or thought as to what is just below the surface, the owner considers it daily. Patiently he waits for the day the ground responds to the warmth of the sun. From the time the seeds are planted, much thought and preparation go toward the reaping of the harvest. If the owner of the field does not have enough workers on that day, it will be disastrous! The image of the field is a visual reminder to us that our Lord needs workers in His field. When the day of harvest comes, He needs enough workers who know how to reap the new life He has planted.

Similarly, imagine a nursery so large you are unable to see the end or the beginning of its length or width. This nursery is filled to capacity with infants and toddlers in need of care. And yet not enough adults are there to care for the little ones. Rather, small children are running around trying to give what little care and comfort they can. Can you imagine such a scary scene? It sends shivers up and down my spine to picture precious little children neglected because there are not enough mature workers to care for them.

The Lord showed me this visual image and said, "If My children do not grow up, then babies will have to take care of the new babies about to be born!" We are not far from the time when millions upon millions will be saved and added to the Church. If we do not grow up for Christ's sake and for the sake of the soon-coming harvest, the new life will have to take care of the new life. Millions of new believers will not be properly held, loved, nurtured and taught if we do not prepare for the approaching need.

How sad for these little ones if they are not comforted and healed of pain brought by the messes their lives have made because no one was there to help change them! Even with salvation freely flowing, without someone to feed them, starvation is sure to destroy or stunt their growth and development. If that happens, they will never come to the full knowledge of God or grow to the full stature of Christ. The little toddlers who think they are all grown up might try to pick up an infant, tire from their attempt to care for it and simply drop the child! Eyes would be poked, preventing clear vision or even causing blindness. There would be many casualties. This is certainly not God's intention for the great ingathering of new believers.

> His intention was the perfecting and the full equipping of the saints (His consecrated people), [that they should do] the work of ministering toward building up Christ's body (the church), [That it might develop] until we all attain oneness in the faith and in the comprehension of the [full and accurate] knowledge of the Son of God, that [we might arrive] at really mature manhood (the completeness of personality which is nothing less than the standard height of Christ's own perfection), the measure of the stature of the fullness of the Christ and the completeness found in Him.
>
> Ephesians 4:12–13

Paul goes on to say, "So then, we may no longer be children, tossed [like ships] to and fro between chance gusts of teaching and wavering with every changing wind of doctrine" (Ephesians 4:14). Once we have become mature in the Lord and have achieved the full measure of the stature of Christ, then we will no longer be "[the prey of] the cunning and cleverness of unscrupulous men" who invent errors to mislead us. Because our lives have been brought to the maturity of Christ's love, they will "lovingly express truth in all things." We will speak truly, deal truly and live truly. Our lives will be "enfolded in love"! Paul exhorts, "Let us grow up in every way and in all things into Him Who is the Head, [even] Christ (the Messiah, the Anointed One)" (Ephesians 4:15).

Jehosheba Answered the Question and the Call

The Bible tells us of one woman in particular who answered both the question and the call. Her story begins when

42-year-old Ahaziah ruled as king of Jerusalem for one year before he was killed in battle. During his reign, the Bible says he walked in the ways of his grandfather, wicked King Ahab. Ahab practiced evil in the sight of the Lord, provoking Him to anger more than all the kings of Israel before him (see 1 Kings 16:30–33). King Ahaziah also took counsel from his mother, Athaliah, to do wickedly (see 2 Chronicles 22:3). Although Ahaziah was made king of Judah, Athaliah was able to control the country by controlling her son. Then when Athaliah discovered her son was dead, she made sure her control would continue by doing the unthinkable: destroying all the royal family of Judah and establishing herself as ruler over Jerusalem!

While this terrible massacre was taking place, our heroine answered God's call on her life to be a mother in the house. "Jehosheba, the daughter of the king, took Joash [infant] son of Ahaziah and stole him away from among the king's sons who were to be slain, and she put him and his nurse in a bedchamber. So Jehosheba daughter of King Jehoram, sister of Ahaziah, and wife of Jehoiada the priest, hid [Joash] from [his grandmother] Athaliah, so that she did not slay him" (2 Chronicles 22:11). Joash was hidden in the house of God for six years while his grandmother ruled over the land.

But in the seventh year, the priest courageously made a covenant with the captains of hundreds to overthrow Athaliah's wicked dictatorship and proclaim little Joash king! They gathered together priests from all the cities and chiefs of the fathers' houses of Israel and came to Jerusalem. "And all the assembly made a covenant in the house of God with the king [little Joash, to suddenly proclaim his sovereignty and overthrow Athaliah's tyranny]. And Jehoiada the priest said to them, Behold, the king's son shall reign, as the Lord has said of the offspring of David" (2 Chronicles 23:3).

A third of the priests and Levites stood as doorkeepers, another third stood at the king's house and the final third waited at the foundation gate. Jehoiada set all the rest of the people in the courts of the house of the Lord as a guard for the king, "every man having his weapon (missile) in his hand, from the right side to the left side of the temple, around the altar and the temple. Then they brought out the king's son and put the crown on him and gave him the testimony or law and made him king" (2 Chronicles 23:10–11). Of all things, Athaliah had the audacity to scream, "Treason!" Then when she ran for her life, she was overthrown and killed (see verses 13–15).

After that, Joash reigned forty years. Although he forsook righteousness and just dealing near the end of his life, Joash did what was right in the sight of God all the days of Jehoiada the priest, his uncle, and he repaired the house of the Lord (see 2 Chronicles 24:2–4).

Protecting the Seed

When Jehosheba interfered with the new queen's mandate, she was not an outsider or even a servant in the palace—she was a daughter of the king. Her brother was King Ahaziah, and their father had been King Jehoram, the husband of wicked Athaliah. Athaliah was a descendant of Queen Jezebel, who was known for wickedly manipulating her husband, King Ahab, so she could control the nation. Queen Jezebel worshiped the Baals and sought to destroy the prophets of God, especially Elijah. Athaliah had been mentored well in wickedness—Jezebel's same ruthless spirit was operating in her!

Jehosheba, however, was of a different Spirit. She was a godly woman of royalty who, because of her love for God, refused to be mentored in the ways of the women before her. She chose God's Word for her counsel, and His Word became her strength for righteousness and her hope for peace. When great wickedness reigned and others were immobilized by fear, Jehosheba rose up against control and injustice and as *a mother in the house* saved the infant as if he were her own.

If she had been caught defying Athaliah, Jehosheba would have lost her life. Yet because she loved righteousness and hated wickedness, she chose to do something about it. Jehosheba trusted and hoped that one day the people would find salvation and peace through the king's infant son.

Like Jehosheba, we need to make ourselves ready and prepare ourselves for the salvation of millions! We also have a "Son" to proclaim as king!

> For God so greatly loved and dearly prized the world that He [even] gave up His only begotten (unique) Son, so that whoever believes in (trusts in, clings to, relies on) Him shall not perish (come to destruction, be lost) but have eternal (everlasting) life. For God did not send the Son into the world in order to judge (to reject, to condemn, to pass sentence on) the world, but that the world might find salvation and be made safe and sound through Him.
>
> John 3:16–17

The Son of God was born, grew, died for our sins, rose from the dead and imparted His Spirit to all who believe in Him. Because of this we, too—like Jehosheba—can have a different Spirit. Like her, we have the power to take action against injustice. We can let our hearts trust and hope for peace. It does not matter what kind of upbringing we have had or what our past might have been: If we believe that Jesus is King, we must also pick up the promise and purposes of God. We must run with Him, hide Him in the temple of our hearts and proclaim His Kingdom to the nations!

Are You Willing to Be a Jehosheba?

The great harvest is going to bring more people into the Kingdom of God than any other time in history. The importance and urgency of the hour outweighs anyone making a name for himself or herself, looking successful or drawing people to a particular church building or program. The Father's call is all about the love of God and His heart for souls. The day of preparing and teaching others to prepare for God's end-time harvest is at hand. The Father's desire is for us to come to full maturity so we might reproduce His life in others. The call for mentors is not about control; it is about encouraging, developing and releasing hearts to effectively love and serve the King.

A mother prepares and teaches her children how to live and function within their home and society. She teaches them how to use tools to effectively accomplish and fulfill responsibilities in life, to study hard, manage a household or family, do laundry, vacuum, cook and be given to hospitality. In the same manner, God wants the older woman to teach others how to use tools of love, wisdom, knowledge, understanding and discretion so they can live and function in the Kingdom of God.

Are you willing to be a Jehosheba? Are you willing to lay down your life to rescue those sentenced to death? Are you willing to care for them, teach them and put the Word of God into their hands?

God is calling us to make changes in our lives and lifestyles so we can be working models and vehicles of His purposes. I believe the Lord is telling the older women who have walked faithfully with Him, "Daughter, your job is not finished! It is time to help prepare the younger women for what is ahead. It is time to encourage them in faithful service. It is time to be like a midwife, helping young women give birth to their gifts. Tell them, 'It won't be long. Hang in there!' It is time to teach them to love Me, as well as the people I place in their lives. It is time to tell those going through fiery trials, 'I know it's hot, but it's worth it.' It is time to exhort: 'Hold on to humility. Embrace it. Work hard at it so you don't fall!' It is time to teach others how to carry My presence to the world."

God is raising up spiritual daughters to display His glory. He is calling us out of complacency and up out of defeat. He has given us the same glory the Father has given to Christ, so that we might move in the same anointing. His intention is that we love and nurture the coming harvest and that we teach righteousness to those who are gathered into the House of the Lord.

Because of the urgency of the hour and for the sake of His harvest, the voice of God is calling, *Is there a mother in the house?*

4

THE ROLE OF WOMEN
IN THE CHURCH

THE CHURCH IS full of controversy concerning women in ministry today. These discussions exist at different levels and degrees, and while some arguments might seem valid, a greater concern should be that too many women are sitting idle within the Church and feeling like second-class citizens!

Certainly God has established order concerning the role of women within the Church and at home, but undue worry about appearing out of order, overbearing or usurping has become a bondage to many women in the Body of Christ. Those who have been overly concerned about what others think regarding their devotion to God have become spiritually frustrated. Many feel misunderstood, even concerning their motives in wanting to serve Him. Because some women are afraid they might step out of line in regard to this debatable subject, they have chosen instead to sit and wait until they learn what their place in the Church and world is.

This dormancy is certainly not God's intention for His daughters. In fact, it is nothing less than a strategy and trick of the devil to keep women inactive, for we live in the most crucial days in all of history—the threshold of the great and mighty harvest—and the Lord needs us to be doing His work!

Walking in Fear and Complacency

As women lie dormant in the Church, two situations result:

1. Women are being held back from doing God's will.
2. Women are holding themselves back because of fear.

Walking in fear also can cause us to embrace a spirit of complacency. Eventually complacency causes us to become frustrated and angry because we are not walking and living out the call God has for our lives.

First John 4:18 says, "There is no fear in love [dread does not exist], but full-grown (complete, perfect) love turns fear out of doors and expels every trace of terror! For fear brings with it the thought of punishment, and [so] he who is afraid has not reached the full maturity of love [is not yet grown into love's complete perfection]." Women are beginning to exchange the spirit of complacency for a spirit of tenacity that is moving them toward God's purposes. Women's hearts are searching to know and understand the liberty Christ's love has bought them. They desire to learn what their individual roles in serving Him might be, and they are choosing to grow up in Christ!

What do I mean when I say grow up in Christ? It has nothing to do with how long we have known the Lord, the level of knowledge we have or in which various gifts of the Spirit we operate. The maturity of Christ found in us is measured by the degree of *love* we are free to express through our lives.

Today God is calling His daughters from a background mentality to an up-front, hands-on commission to do the work Jesus has appointed them to do. He is stirring, healing and emboldening women's hearts to believe and to trust the Spirit of God residing in them. The dissatisfaction of having a form of godliness without God's tangible presence and power in their lives is mounting in the hearts of women. They are turning from complacency and instead are seeking to intimately know God and His purpose for their existence.

The Biblical Example of Women in Service to Jesus

During the three and a half years Jesus ministered on earth as a man, many women followed His ministry. They devoted their time to serving Him, as well as His twelve disciples:

> Soon afterward, [Jesus] went on through towns and villages, preaching and bringing the good news (the Gospel) of the kingdom of God. And the Twelve [apostles] were with Him, And also some women who had been cured of evil spirits and diseases: Mary, called Magdalene, from whom seven demons had been expelled; And Joanna, the wife of Chuza, Herod's household manager; and Susanna; and many others, who ministered to and provided for Him and them out of their property and personal belongings.
>
> Luke 8:1–3

These women did not join up with the Jesus Team for what they could get but rather for what they could give. Each woman gave from her own possessions, finances and time for the work and ministry of Christ. I am convinced their motive was love and that their intensity for God emboldened and freed them to step out of their conventional and predictable roles within a man's world and culture.

Because of their love and gratefulness to the Lord, they pursued Jesus to minister to Him. These women who ministered to and for the Lord were women of all social classes—from the ex-prostitute who at one time had an undesirable disposition to the responsible married woman with a prestigious job in the king's palace. Yet they worked side by side, relating to one another as friends and sisters in Christ. Because they did not shrink back in fear but made themselves available for service, Jesus released and entrusted them to the cutting-edge ministry of what the Father was doing. He highly esteemed them and the work they did in the Kingdom. These women are God's example for us today to emulate, and the blessing He bestowed on them because of their faithfulness can be ours as well.

Deborah Arose, a Mother in Israel

Chapters 4 and 5 of the book of Judges offer two more biblical examples of women who made themselves available for service in the Kingdom. God chose to use them to perform the particular jobs He had for them to do at a particular time, for the sake of the glory of His name.

While Joshua and all the elders who had seen the great works of the Lord were alive, the people served God. But when that generation died "there arose another generation after them who did not know (recognize, understand) the Lord, or even the work which He had done for Israel" (Judges 2:10). Instead they forsook the Lord and served other gods. The Israelites fell repeatedly into apostasy and then oppression as invading nations exploited them economically. As tribe after tribe went into their individual, inherited and appointed lands, they failed to drive out the inhabitants as the Lord had commanded them to do.

> Now the Angel of the Lord went up from Gilgal to Bochim. And He said, I brought you up from Egypt and have brought you to the land which I swore to give to your fathers, and I said, I will never break My covenant with you; And you shall make no covenant with the inhabitants of this land; but you shall break down their altars. But you have not obeyed My voice. Why have you done this? So now I say, I will not drive them out from before you; but they shall be as thorns in your sides, and their gods shall be a snare to you. When the Angel of the Lord spoke these words to all the Israelites, the people lifted up their voice and wept. They named that place Bochim [weepers], and they sacrificed there to the Lord.
>
> Judges 2:1–5

God had commanded Israel to love the Lord with all of its heart, mind and might. He commanded the parents to do this first, and then they were to teach and impress these things diligently upon the hearts and minds of their children—not weekly, but from the time they got up in the morning until they went to bed at night. God had forewarned them concerning this vital commandment. He told them that if they did not obey, then after they had entered the Promised Land their children would grow up and forget the Lord and go after false gods (see Deuteronomy 6:4–15). Because the Israelites were not careful to do what God had commanded them to do, an entire nation became ignorant of the knowledge of God and His blessings could not be upon them. The anger of the Lord was kindled against the children of Israel, and He gave them into the power of plunderers who robbed them and sold them into the hands of the enemies who surrounded them. Judges 2:15 says, "They were bitterly distressed."

Because of the Lord's covenant with His people, however, He raised up judges, or leaders, who would deliver them out of the hands of those who robbed them. Yet they did not listen to their judges! When the Lord raised up judges for them, He was with the judge and delivered them from their oppression. But when the judge died, they turned away from God and corrupted themselves even more than their fathers had. They refused to turn their hearts to God but continued their evil practices and stubborn ways. Because of this, the Lord said He would no longer drive out their enemies from before them.

The Lord raised up a judge named Othniel to deliver them, and afterward the land had peace for forty years. But when Othniel died, the people again turned against God and entered into oppression for eighteen years. Then they cried out to God, who raised up another deliverer named Ehud. Ehud delivered the children of Israel, and afterward the land had peace for eighty years. But after Ehud died, the people once again turned to other gods and the Lord sold them into the hand of Jabin, king of Canaan. The commander of Jabin's army was Sisera. He had nine hundred iron chariots and severely oppressed the people for twenty years! Again the children of Israel cried out to the Lord for deliverance, and He answered them.

This time God gave them Deborah, the wife of Lappidoth, to judge Israel. Deborah, who was also a prophetess, was content to sit under a palm tree, where the people came to her for counsel and judgment. But when God called her to battle alongside the mighty men of God, then "Deborah, arose—a mother in Israel" (Judges 5:7).

Judges 4:6–7 tells us that she sent for Barak, a mighty warrior, saying, "Has not the Lord, the God of Israel, commanded [you], Go, gather your men at Mount Tabor, taking 10,000 men from the tribes of Naphtali and Zebulun? And I will draw out Sisera, the general of Jabin's army, to meet you at the river Kishon with his chariots and his multitude, and I will deliver him into your hand?"

Deborah was asking Barak a question! Evidently Deborah had previously prophesied the word of the Lord to Barak, and he had not yet done what God had told him to do. Barak's reply was, "If you will go with me, then I will go; but if you will not go with me, I will not go" (verse 8). Deborah agreed to go into battle alongside Barak. Then she prophesied further to him regarding the battle, saying the glory and victory would not be given to him but to a woman.

I have heard people refer to Barak as a wimp, but I do not believe he was cowardly at all! He had seen the strength and power of Sisera's army, and he knew the limitations of his own. I am sure he had logical reservations about taking only ten thousand footmen to fight against Sisera's multitude with iron chariots. His question was probably, "Are you *sure* you heard from God?" It would be disastrous for Deborah to miss the mark on that one! It is also obvious that Barak's confidence in God, as well as his personal relationship with Him, was not strong, but he was convinced that Deborah's was. If Deborah agreed to go, it meant she was certain God promised victory to the army of Israel. Barak, as well as all Israel, had witnessed God's hand

and anointing upon her life. He knew that Deborah's presence assured God's presence.

When the battle was over and the victory won, Deborah and Barak rejoiced in a duet together. In their song, they told the complete story of their great adventure and victory in detail. They defined Deborah's position and place of authority in Israel: "The villages were unoccupied and rulers ceased in Israel until you arose—you, Deborah, arose—a mother in Israel" (Judges 5:7). When oppression overtook every dwelling place and no capable or qualified person was found to rule God's people, God discovered one who feared and obeyed Him—and Deborah arose!

Just like Deborah, our presence also can guarantee God's presence if we love Him and obey His commands. Wherever we go, His presence will minister peace and execute judgment upon the oppressor of our souls. Because God saw a willing heart that was pure before Him, the Lord lifted Deborah up to be a mouthpiece of His law and a mother who loved and led His children to righteousness. It was not a small task that God entrusted to her, for Deborah did not just rule a tribe or a city—she ruled a nation!

At the end of the victory song, Deborah and Barak sang, "So let all Your enemies perish, O Lord! But let those who love Him be like the sun when it rises in its might" (Judges 5:31).

Another Willing Heart: Jael

"And the Lord confused and terrified Sisera and all his chariot drivers and all his army before Barak with the sword. And Sisera alighted from his chariot and fled on foot" (Judges 4:15).

Sisera ran toward the tent of Jael, the wife of Heber, a Kenite. Heber had been at peace with King Jabin, so Sisera thought his tent might be a safe place to hide. Before Sisera ever got to the tent, Jael ran up the road to meet him and invited him to hide there. After he gratefully entered, Jael quickly covered him with a rug.

Because he was thirsty and worn out from running, he uncovered his head and asked Jael for some water to drink. She was more than gracious and gave him warm milk instead to help him rest from his exhausting escape. He instructed her to stand at the door of the tent to watch for Barak, and she covered him again. Sisera commanded her that if anyone came to inquire about him, she should say he was not there.

It was not long before Sisera was in a deep sleep. While he was snoring, Jael quietly and softly approached him with a tent pin and hammer in her hand. With a sudden blow, Jael nailed Sisera's head to the ground! When Barak arrived looking for Sisera, Jael came out of her tent to meet him saying, "Come, and I will show you the man you seek" (Judges 4:22).

Because Jael had become fed up with injustice in the land, she was not fearful or easily intimidated. She was not a self-centered woman who was satisfied having peace and security in her own home while others were troubled on every side. Her determined heart was for peace in the land, and that pursuit emboldened her to go out to meet the enemy! When she found a chance to make a difference for righteousness, she seized her opportunity to do so.

In Deborah and Barak's song of victory they blessed Jael, who was not indecisive or unsure about her involvement. They blessed her above others, singing: "Blessed above women shall Jael, the wife of Heber the Kenite, be; blessed shall she be above women in the tent. [Sisera] asked for water, and she gave him milk; she brought him curds in a lordly dish. She put her [left] hand to the tent pin, and her right hand to the workmen's hammer. And with the wooden hammer she smote Sisera, she smote his head, yes, she struck and pierced his temple. He sank, he fell, he lay still at her feet. At her feet he sank, he fell; where he sank, there he fell—dead!" (Judges 5:24–27).

Why a Woman?

I have heard different explanations as to why God at times has chosen a woman rather than a man for His service. The most common is: "Well, God will use a woman when He can't find a man to do the job."

Isn't it interesting that God never apologized or even explained His decision to anoint a woman to the office of prophet—a spokesperson of God and for God? He has left many scratching their heads, wondering why He would appoint a woman to lead an entire nation! God also did not elaborate on why He allowed the glory for extreme bravery and national victory to be given to a woman.

God's thinking concerning leadership is obvious in these first five chapters of the book of Judges. His choice is determined by an obedient and yielded heart—not by gender. Only almighty God ordered Deborah's steps, choosing, appointing and raising her up. Deborah was a woman, a wife, a prophetess and a judge, and she also became a warrior. Deborah was not related to national leaders like Moses and Aaron as Miriam had been, but Deborah knew her God and because of that she was strong in spirit and ministered with authority and power! Nowhere is it recorded that Deborah was overbearing and controlling. Nowhere is it recorded that because of her gender, Deborah was fearful, intimidated or backward. Her rule was born out of her relationship with God and out of her willingness to answer the call of God on her life as a mother to the people she served.

But Deborah was not the only woman God used to accomplish His work! Jael was willing to answer His call, too. Evidently Jael did not feel it was her place to remain indoors just because she was a woman while the men fought the war. Just as a mother would risk her own safety for the sake of her children, Jael was willing to risk her life so others might know peace and prosperity. Because Jael was a willing volunteer who gave herself as an offering to the Lord, God sold Sisera into the hands of a woman (see Judges 5:2)!

Perhaps in one sense it is true that God will use women when no men step up to the plate. In their victory song, Deborah and Barak questioned where the tribes were when their country was going to war. The clan of Reuben was indecisive in their hearts about fighting the enemy, and Deborah and Barak said that Reuben's men lingered among their sheepfolds just listening to the baaing of the sheep. They sang about Gilead remaining beyond the Jordan instead of enlisting for war. They asked why Dan stayed with the ships and Asher sat still on the seacoast and remained by his creeks instead of going to battle for God's people. And Zebulun and Naphtali had endangered their lives to the death. Deborah and Barak's song honored not only the men of the tribes of Israel, but these two women who were willing to be used for the purposes of the Kingdom. "For the leaders who took the lead in Israel, for the *people* who offered themselves willingly, bless the Lord!" (Judges 5:2, emphasis added). This time women were the leaders who took the lead and gave themselves willingly. This was the only requirement for God to give them His power and authority.

Throughout the Word of God and throughout history, women have accomplished extraordinary exploits. Amazing miracles have been performed through fragile but willing vessels of His precious daughters, and many have laid down their lives for the Kingdom.

If you have questioned your role as a woman in the Church or your level of anointing, look at Matthew 10:8. Jesus commanded His disciples, saying, "Cure the sick, raise the dead, cleanse the lepers, drive out demons. Freely (without pay) you have received, freely (without charge) give." God is not a respecter of only one gender. He is not looking only for men who will serve His purposes, but for all *mankind* to love Him and to commit their lives to doing His will. Our Father has not withheld ministry from His daughters but has released His authority and power to them.

What God is looking for is a willing volunteer!

The Battle Requires Both Men and Women

Years ago in prayer God gave me a vision of an intense and heated battle. Godly men were on the front lines warring against Satan and his troops. Suddenly women began to move toward the front line to take their places beside the men. The women were not clothed in army fatigues but in radiant, dazzling gowns that represented the beauty of holiness and the righteousness of God upon their lives. As the women drew near to the front line, the men turned to watch them approach. Their faces revealed gratefulness, and they quickly stretched out their hands and placed and positioned the women beside them.

When Satan saw these women coming in the beauty and glory of Christ he doubled over, pulled at his hair and screamed, "Oh, no! Here they come again!" Then as the women were given their rightful positions on the front line, he turned and fled.

Satan knows that when the Body of Christ comes together in perfect unity no power or force can withstand it. Truly, power and authority that are yet to come will be released as both genders unite in the purposes of God.

Ministry in the Shadows

Some time ago I received a special edition from *The Voice of the Martyrs* magazine that pertained to women in restricted nations who are effectively serving the King. The issue was dedicated to Sabina Wurmbrand (1913–2000), a woman who ministered in the shadows of persecution. She inspired her sisters in Christ worldwide by reminding them that they are the "pupil of [God's] eye" (Psalm 17:8).

The following is taken and quoted from that magazine, one to which I think every Christian should subscribe. It certainly pulled my head out of the sand, reminding and encouraging me in the purpose for my existence—to love God, love others and to save those who are eternally lost in sin. It reminded me to pray for wisdom, strength and protection over my Christian family worldwide, and it motivated me to work while I am able.

They are mothers, sisters and daughters. They are breadwinners. They are pastors and teachers. They evangelize and build churches. And they minister under some of the most extreme circumstances in the world today.

Who are they?

They are our sisters in Christ in restricted nations around the globe.

China, Sudan, Vietnam, Iran and Saudi Arabia are just a few of the nations where these women are not only rejected for knowing Christ but are also considered social cast-offs for being who they are—women. Yet despite these cultural and political pressures, they are carefully tucked under the shelter of God's wings where many effectively minister in the shadows because they know that they are, as David fittingly wrote, the "apple of God's eye"—the object of His favor.

Our desire is to draw attention to an often overlooked part of Christ's Body—the women who bravely and faithfully minister the Gospel in nations hostile to it. Some of these women respectfully wear the black veil mandated by Islamic law so they do not draw unnecessary attention to themselves as they walk to house church meetings. Some work tirelessly in rice fields to provide for their families so their husbands can be free to evangelize. And some are left to pastor the flocks while their husbands spend time in prison for their ministries.

I want to describe what I saw as I looked at some of the pictures distributed throughout the magazine. First I noticed a beautiful *woman* from Bangladesh holding a Bible under her arms. Her face radiated joy and peace. I read the caption, which told me the people in Bangladesh are often attacked when they convert to Christianity. Then deep within the delta of an isolated village, they train to make themselves ready to share the Gospel with their attackers.

In the jungles and cities of Southeast Asia, where governments oppose church construction, a picture depicts eleven *women* cramped together in a small, poorly constructed home. There they worship God and fervently pray together for souls.

In China, Laos and Vietnam, Christians are beaten, houses are burned and many are imprisoned. Yet a picture reveals several *women* joyously smiling because they have been equipped and prepared to share the Gospel with others. I saw a picture of a Vietnamese pastor and his *wife* taking the Gospel to hungry souls by night, as fishers of men traveling through water and mud. Another picture shows a man standing in water. With him are five *women* climbing out of the water with boxes of Christian books upon their backs that will be distributed throughout China. Another photo shows an elderly *woman* printing Christian books in a cave. She patiently prepares these Christian books in secret—sewing them by hand! Although police discovered that press, the article tells us that printing continues in other places.

In the midst of a holy war and persecution, several Sudanese *women* work to help unload a Voice of the Martyrs airplane that is filled with blankets and boxes of aid. Above that picture, *women* are sitting together with the Word of God in their hands. Another snapshot reveals a beautiful young *girl* reading her Bible. Yet if attacked and captured, they all might be raped and sold into slavery.

Because of their intense love for God, women in these restricted nations not only minister the Gospel but also are willing to lay down their lives for His name's sake and for the sake of His Kingdom. This special edition ends by thanking the reader for joining them on a journey into the lives of our sisters in Christ who selflessly and sacrificially "minister in the shadows" in restricted nations. Their prayer is that we in the free world would be inspired to take up His cross as well, despite the cultural and social pressures facing women in the Body of Christ today.

A Willing Volunteer

I remember one particular dinner with Jill Austin, founder of Master Potter Ministries. As we ate, she looked me in the eye and said, "God has called you to take a stand for women in ministry. Are you willing to pay the price?"

Jokingly I stuck my fingers in my ears and sang "La-la-la-la!" to drown out her words. I told her that I knew paying the price meant criticism and having my heart misjudged—just because I am a woman. I felt I had already paid somewhat of a price. I was not sure I wanted to go there again!

Her response was in the form of two questions: "Are you willing to be a forerunner, paving the way for God's daughters? And if not, are you willing to forfeit what your daughters *will* accomplish for God?"

I was serious when I replied that I definitely wanted to accomplish everything the Father has destined for me to do. And yes, I will take a stand and even lay down my life to see God's daughters come forth in His purposes.

Like Mary Magdalene, Martha and the other women who ministered to Christ, like Deborah and Jael, like those women in restricted nations in the world today, I am willing to be a volunteer. I am willing to be a mother in God's Kingdom.

Releasing Women's Hearts
for Service

If each of us would step out of ourselves to give away what we have received, then the Church would develop in maturity much more rapidly. We would experience and see with our very eyes the power and unity the early Church had. Theirs was a relationship of true teamwork encompassed by their love for God, their love for one another and their passion to do the will of the Father.

But too many of God's daughters are held back from operating in the way God wants them to operate. They feel inadequate, foolish and unsure because their pasts have been progressions of broken dreams, broken hearts and broken lives.

I believe the majority of God's daughters are in great need of validation and acceptance concerning their role in Christianity.

Those who have been wounded by religion, human reasoning, opinions and fables are in need of truth and healing so they can seize their destinies in Christ. They desire to be developed and released to do the works of Jesus and are hungry to learn, grow and be built up by someone who has gone before them. Because very little mentoring has been done, the majority of God's daughters have been left to learn and figure out practical wisdom on their own. Many of them look to secular magazines, TV and their own human wisdom for counsel and direction for their lives, and then they wonder why they are unfulfilled and lacking in joy.

My mother-in-law, Wanda Sustar, is someone who has spent years pouring her life into others. Concerning God's desire to establish His daughters in His purposes, God recently spoke to her and said, *Don't let yourself be deceived! There are broken women everywhere you go, and many women have been wounded and broken by even their own mothers!*

Like never before, the hearts of women are crying out to be mentored in the ways of Christ. The younger woman is looking for someone older who is not afraid to step out and say, "I've been there! I've done that! Let me tell you what I've discovered." These younger women especially need the example and ministry of older women who live, move and have their being in Christ. They desire to know and understand what God wants them to do and how He requires them to behave and relate to others.

Answering God's Call to Compassion

The older woman who has held fast to God is sound and strong in spirit. Because of her depth of intimacy with the Lord, she is able to impart the truth, wisdom and knowledge of God.

Many older women, however, hold to a common deception. Because they cannot relate to brokenness, need or a shameful past that many women have experienced, they feel unqualified in wisdom and understanding. But the truth is that God does not require us to relate to specific pain, needs or sins. He only requires that we make ourselves available and give what we have received.

For fourteen years I ministered to women who had undergone abortions. While I led the post-abortion ministry, 100 percent of the women receiving counsel experienced 100 percent healing and restoration through Jesus Christ. I also was honored to help establish the first Crisis Pregnancy Center in France and was the main speaker in Linz, Austria, for a citywide meeting on abortion. Because these areas of ministry were once listed on my bio sketch, wherever I traveled women who had experienced abortions would approach me for counsel and prayer.

Because I have understanding and compassion for these women, many people have assumed I have had an abortion. I have not. Why, then, did I embark upon that particular ministry? How could I understand the pain and trauma these women have experienced when I have not experienced them myself? The answer to those questions is that the Lord simply called me to touch these women with the love, forgiveness and healing of God, and I answered His call.

God wants to bring restoration and edification to all His daughters. He wants them to experientially know the power, strength and healing that He offers. In His presence, all my criticism, judgment and debate about the issue of abortion vanished and His mercy, grace and compassion filled my heart for these women and their families. Even though I have had no personal experience with abortion, I have made other mistakes concerning wrong choices. Because of those mistakes, I have also known sorrow and grief. So I can only imagine the sense of buyer's remorse after having purchased an abortion. At times my heart has almost broken over the sorrow, fear and rejection these women have experienced.

My responsibility to God's call of ministering to these women was to answer it. But in doing so, I had to study His Word, as well as anything pertaining to abortion that I could get my hands on. I wanted to show myself approved unto God; and I wanted not simply knowledge but also understanding (see Proverbs 4:7 and 2 Timothy 2:15).

The results I witnessed were not because I was a great counselor but because I looked to, followed and spoke the words of the one and only true Counselor (see Isaiah 9:6)! We may not be able to identify with specific sins, but we all can identify with human reasoning that leads to destruction (see Proverbs 14:12). We all can identify with failure, heartbreak, disappointment and the weaknesses of mankind. If we will have the compassion and love Christ has for us, then we will be effective ministers and mothers in the Kingdom of God.

Mothering: A Call to Love and Lay Down One's Life

Lattie McDonough is a prophet with a seasoned ministry. He and his wife, Barbara, have been a spiritual father and mother to many. Not too long ago I had a conversation with Barbara. As she spoke, it was obvious she desired to do for others what Christ had done for her.

Barbara told me about different friends God had brought into her life throughout the years. She had found it a delight and honor to carry their burdens in both practical and spiritual ways. She held them dear to her heart and spoke of how they often served one another. She said she loved them so much that she would do anything for them! I enjoyed hearing about her relationships with other women, and as she was talking she suddenly stopped and looked directly into my eyes. With a serious tone she said, "I love you, too, Shirley—and I will fight for you! If you are ever in need, call me."

What a blessing that moment was to my heart! It strengthened me to know that this mature woman in Christ loved me so much that she would immediately engage in warfare through prayer over God's purpose for my life. It helped me to remember that true Christian love makes us active in service and effective in ministry.

As our passion for God increases, the burden of the Lord also increases within us, causing us to embrace His passion for souls. It motivates us to reach beyond ourselves, to gather others to the Lord and to point them to His will for their lives. Having a deep relationship with the Lord and others frees us simply to do whatever we see the Father doing within the relational sphere in which He places us. "By this we come to know (progressively to recognize, to perceive, to understand) the [essential] love: that He laid down His [own] life for us; and we ought to lay [our] lives down for [those who are our] brothers [in Him]" (1 John 3:16). Barbara understands God's loving, relational approach to leadership, and this understanding motivates her to reach beyond herself and to point others to the Lord's will for their lives.

I believe we all need to examine ourselves to see if we are sensitive to others around us. Do we understand their insecurities? Do we understand their fears? Do we understand their brokenness? Or are we critical of their weaknesses because our focus is on ourselves or on our important work or even on our own need to get a job done? We show that we understand God's love by laying down our lives for others.

Love and kindness toward others is demonstrated through humility, not through thinking higher of ourselves than we ought. Since God is love and love endures long, is patient and is kind (see 1 John 4:8 and 1 Corinthians 13:4) and since God's Spirit dwells in us, shouldn't these attributes be evident and affect everything we do?

Those older, mature women in Christ—like Barbara—who say from their hearts, "Here I am, Lord. Fill me, use me, pour me out. I will go where You want me to go. I will do what You want me to do. I will be what You want me to be," will experience God's favor and walk in His anointing. Their lives will be given to the task of setting souls free, just as God is doing.

What Happens When Older Women Do Not Mentor

Throughout the Church today, perhaps simply through ignorance rather than disobedience, many older women are not answering the call of God to mentor the younger women. Due to traditions, mindsets and insecurities, this is simply the way it has been. Because of this, it has been far too common for ministers of the male gender to counsel, teach and train young Christian women concerning their relationships and ministries. When this happens, an inherent danger raises its ugly head: the danger of sexual sin.

Over the past decades we have watched (and have been embarrassed as the world has also seen) a great falling into sexual sin among many of the leaders God has appointed—primarily men. Of course, until Christ returns, we will have among us misleading talkers and deceivers whose intention is for their own personal gain; but I am convinced that most of those who have fallen were genuine men of God called by God to watch over His flock.

Male ministers who have kept themselves pure might feel a bit defensive at the writing of this. They might feel unjustly attacked or falsely accused in their motive to minister to young women. I am sure the majority of men who are servants of God minister to women out of a sincere love and devotion to God's service, and many pastors do not have older women who are mature and able to train the younger women of their churches. But the fact still holds that adultery has become a widespread epidemic among Christian leaders today, and it is imperative that we examine and reevaluate what we have been doing.

Women whose hearts have been misunderstood or broken often crave tender understanding from the opposite sex. A male minister who is gentle and compassionate toward her could unknowingly capture her heart. Even though he might be a man of integrity, be morally upright and have a sincere desire to help this young woman, his tender compassion could cause her to stumble. This is why women sometimes become infatuated and fall in love with their doctors, counselors or pastors.

In many cases, the *personal* ministry from a man to a woman does more harm than good! Infatuation usually comes suddenly upon a woman, and its effects bring increased guilt and despair, adding to the degree of bondage in which she already finds herself. Becoming involved in an illegitimate relationship, whether physical or mental, can only damage her already-wounded spirit!

Scripture Offers a Safeguard

So what has been the problem?

I believe we are reaping the results of ignoring an essential safeguard God set for His Church, which is found in the book of Titus. The apostle Paul left Titus, his spiritual son, in charge of the believers living in Crete. This church had not only been unorganized, but also its members needed much admonition. Concerning the raising up and releasing of ministers over the flock, Paul instructs Titus in a letter. From Paul's letter the essential elements of New Testament theology are taken.

In the very first verse, he states and relates his passion to "stimulate and promote the faith of God's chosen ones and to lead them on to accurate discernment and recognition of and acquaintance with the Truth which belongs to and harmonizes with and tends to godliness" (Titus 1:1).

In the following verses Paul warns Titus about the spreading of wrong doctrine by unscrupulous men (see verses 10–14). Paul speaks about these men who were misleading talkers and self-deceivers. They brought mental stress and subverted whole families with wrong teaching—all for the purpose of getting base advantage and disreputable gain. These men, who called themselves ministers of Christ, were liars, hurtful, idle and lazy gluttons. They taught their traditional myths and fables and were laying down rules made by men to promote their own agendas.

He continues, "To the pure [in heart and conscience] all things are pure, but to the defiled and corrupt and unbelieving nothing is pure; their very minds and consciences are defiled and polluted. They profess to know God [to recognize, perceive, and be acquainted with Him], but deny and disown and renounce Him by what they do; they are detestable and loathsome, unbelieving and disobedient and disloyal and rebellious, and [they are] unfit and worthless for good work (deed or enterprise) of any kind" (Titus 1:15–16).

Paul was bringing to Titus's attention that there are those who call themselves ministers of the Gospel, yet lead the Church by rules, regulations, presumption and sin—not love! Their character and lives are led by the dictates of their own flesh, and they minister and lead others through the power of their own words. Paul said to Titus,

> But [as for] you, teach what is fitting and becoming to sound (wholesome) doctrine [the character and right living that identify true Christians]. Urge the older men to be temperate, venerable (serious), sensible, self-controlled, and sound in the faith, in the love, and in the steadfastness and patience [of Christ].
>
> Titus 2:1–2

First it is important to note here that the doctrine of Christ and the character of Christ must be taught! It is absolutely necessary for godly living. Scripture makes it very clear that our teaching is not to be taught merely by words but also by the life of the one who is doing the teaching. If we are not walking in God's love and living what we are preaching, our words are empty, vain and without power—except to harm or lead astray.

But, secondly, Paul follows this instruction to men with a similar instruction to the older women:

> Bid the older women similarly to be reverent and devout in their deportment as becomes those engaged in sacred service, not slanderers or slaves to drink. They are to give good counsel and be teachers of what is right and noble, So that they will wisely train the young women to be sane and sober of mind (temperate, dis-

ciplined) and to love their husbands and their children, To be self-controlled, chaste, homemakers, good-natured (kindhearted), adapting and subordinating themselves to their husbands, that the word of God may not be exposed to reproach (blasphemed or discredited).

Titus 2:3–5

Just as Paul had mentored or fathered Titus, he was instructing the older women to mentor or mother the younger women in the ways of the Kingdom. He exhorted the older women to teach the young women through counsel and example. Since all things pertaining to life and godliness are met through the full and personal knowledge of Christ Jesus (see 2 Peter 1:3), it is both the spiritual and practical lessons that are needed.

Time for Elder Women to Lead the Younger

God is calling His daughters out of a background mentality to a front-line mentality. He desires that we lay aside self-centeredness and fear and with humility and grace violently take the Kingdom of God by force as a precious prize (see Matthew 11:12)! Our Father is calling forth Titus 2:3–5 women to mentor and equip His daughters for service. Every daughter needs a mother who not only shows her the way, but who is also there to say, "You are doing a great job, honey. I am proud of you!"

You will recall that I shared with you in chapter 1 how the Lord answered my confusion about mothering with the analogy of the two women, one eighty years old and the other sixty. He made it clear to me that maturity is often a different thing than the heart burden to be a mother in the Kingdom of God.

84

Being a mother does not make one mature, nor does it mean everything that a mother does is correct, but it should motivate her to maturity so she can righteously lead others. The standard for her function should be nothing less than that given in Titus 2:3–5. This passage instructs the older women not only to exhibit godly behavior, but also to lead, teach, train and counsel other women in the ways of the Lord. A mother's character must exemplify Christ, not herself. This means that she must grow up for Christ's sake and come to a place of maturity where she can reproduce in others what God has deposited in her. She also must give herself for training. Human reasoning must depart from her life, and instead His wisdom and direction must operate in her so that God's will for His Church and Christ Himself will be glorified. These elder women should be seasoned through experience and through adversity. Can you imagine hiring a physical trainer to get you in shape, yet this trainer herself was not fit? In like manner, the older woman must have a track record of righteous living and be able to teach with her life, as well as from the Word.

God's intention is to bring His espoused Bride to maturity and completeness of personality. Therefore, the ministry of instructing, developing, training and releasing women should not be administered by the elder man, but rather by the elder woman. She is given the task not only of exemplifying Christ, but also of training other women for their development in Christian service. It is time for the elder women to take the younger ones under their wings to bring them to maturity and to the full purpose God has for their lives.

Little of this has been done throughout the Church at large. In this hour, however, a great cry is emanating from the hearts of many women. They are tired of uselessness and living a life of fruitlessness. Today women are looking for older women to mentor and train them for service to God. They know that they are not powerless creatures but effective, hard workers!

Mentors Bring Forth Calling and Destiny

Karen Noe is a minister in her own right who holds responsible positions within her community. She has served as director of the Pregnancy Care Center and on an advisory committee for her area career center. She has held the position of administrative assistant in a computer center for Huntington National Bank, helped establish the first Crisis Pregnancy Center in France and was awarded the outstanding alumni award at an area technical school. Karen has spoken at conferences in her state and abroad and teaches Sunday school at her local church. She is also the adult dance leader, assistant arts team director and my assistant for Women of Royalty Ministries.

Karen did not always know success. Instead hers was a history of brokenness and shame. When she was only three years of age her abusive and alcoholic father abandoned her. Her memories as a child are of her father coming home on the weekends and repeatedly beating her mother. She was a troubled child and teenager, and by the age of 27 she began drinking alcohol every day. Karen believes the very thing that had robbed her life as a child became her god, and because of this her life was on a rapid course of destruction! Karen became involved with a cult that does not believe in heaven, hell or the Savior, Jesus Christ. She knew her choices were wrong but says she was powerless to change herself.

Although she had developed a very close relationship with her mother and a loving relationship with her stepfather, Karen was torn between the love of her family and hatred for herself. Karen began to wonder why anyone would want to stick around in this world and proceeded to plan her own suicide. During that time a professional counselor told Karen that she was beyond hope and without chance of functioning in society. Then on one of the days Karen was strategizing her own death, she fell to her knees, crying out, "Lord, if You are real, take this from me!" Because of the cry of her heart to God, He began a work in her life that day, saving her and transforming her by the renewing of her mind.

While sharing these things before a group of people recently, Karen asked this question: "How can someone with such a horrible past have all the credentials previously shared?" She then answered her own question: "Because God had a plan for my life!"

Karen is a strong advocate for mentoring and credits much of her knowledge and wisdom to different people who mentored her in areas of Christian living. Webster's dictionary defines the word *mentor* as simply "a wise and trusted person." But the British English thesaurus carries the definition further, describing a *mentor* as "a teacher, master, instructor, educator and preceptor." Mentors are those who not only teach but also live by example what they are teaching.

Karen says, "The world's greatness focuses on possession, position and self-sufficiency. Greatness in God's Kingdom, however, is very different. His greatness possesses humility, compassion and anointing. As we are taught and trained in His ways, He brings about His great purpose for our lives. Through the mentors He brings into our lives who are operating in His will, He is able to bring forth the specific calling and destiny He has for each one of us."

I am privileged to be among those whom God chose to help mentor Karen. As a gift, Karen wrote and presented a poem to me in 1991. She says the words are even more alive than they were when she wrote it because she now feels a responsibility to mentor and help guide others along the way to their greatness in Christ.

I feel I've never told you
How much you mean to me.
And although I say I love you,
There's so much more for you to see.

God brought me to you at a time
When my life was so confused.
My past was so bad; my sins were so great;
I felt in His Kingdom I could never be used.

But you brought me new life, a hope and a chance
That someday I would be
A light in this world, a daughter of the King;
Can this new person really be me?

You turned me to Jesus and not to yourself,
Transformed life is what you have prayed.
God heard your prayers and touched my life with grace,
And kept me from going astray.

"Walk with Jesus—it's easy," some people say,
"I don't know why they won't go!"
But people like me need people like you
Because first steps are so hard to know.

I thank God for you and the life I now have
Such peace and joy I have not before known

When I look at my past from the time that we met,
I am amazed at how much I've grown.

A pledge I make: to stand with you
And remain steadfast at your side.
His Kingdom will come and His Will will be done
With Daddy-God as our guide.

This poem helps me to remember not only the value of each individual life but also the unseen potential that lies within each one of us. It helps me to never forget our responsibility to carry the weaknesses of another person and to do all we can to see her restored and made strong.

Arise and Enter the King's Service!

God is calling His daughters to radical holiness and service. He is restoring women's hearts from unsure and broken conditions and calling those whose purpose has been weakened by discouragement or rejection. He is taking them out of a backseat, church-meeting mentality and thrusting them into the highways and byways of life. His purpose for us contains value, security and position. He is releasing His daughters into the King's service!

Like never before, I believe women want to seize their destinies! All are called to salvation, healing, restoration and maturity. All are called to reproduce in others what has been deposited in them. It is time for God's daughters to arise to the purpose for their existence! We must take up the cross of Christ and follow Him. We must give ourselves to training for the service of ministry. We must get up out of ourselves and out of our fears and be released into God's wonderful, redemptive love.

Jesus said, "The harvest is indeed plentiful, but the laborers are few. So pray to the Lord of the harvest to force out and thrust laborers into His harvest" (Matthew 9:37–38).

6

BARREN
NO MORE!

ANY WOMEN HAVE been deceived from entering into
a life of joy, peace and satisfaction in God. They have
surrendered to wounds inflicted upon their souls, to self-pity and
to bitterness. These things, rather than the Word of the Lord,
then become their focus and cause them to become spiritually
barren. In their state of defeat, they find it almost impossible to
lift their heads so they can see beyond their limitations. They
truly suffer, but they also allow their suffering to hinder their
pace until they become immobilized from pursuing God's will
for their lives. These women will never reproduce life in others—only barrenness. Yet God's Word tells us that we have been
appointed (planted) that we might go and bear fruit and keep
on bearing, so that our fruit will remain (see John 15:16). The

Word of God also tells us that those who bear fruit will live and move in power, authority and effective prayer.

This is the day of restoration to the purposes of God. Those who have been barren need someone to help them lift up their eyes and their heads so they can see in faith what God has in store for them and what He wants to do through them. Then they will be *barren no more!*

Hannah—Barren with a Mother's Heart

In days of old the law of the land allowed a man to have more than one wife. Elkanah was such a man. He chose two wives with whom to build his life and family. Elkanah preferred one wife over the other, however, and of course this caused much confusion, hurt and rivalry.

Elkanah's favorite wife was Hannah, who was barren. Even though her barrenness did not really matter to Elkanah, it brought unhappiness, disappointment and confusion to her own heart. Elkanah's other wife, Peninnah, bore him both sons and daughters. Yet her life remained unfilled as well. Although her husband tenderly cared for Peninnah and their children, she was not ignorant to what everyone else knew. It was obvious to anyone who observed their family that Hannah held the strings of her husband's heart and his love for Hannah was much deeper than his love for Peninnah.

This form of marital relationship is hard for most of us to understand, but I am sure we all can imagine the competition and animosity Peninnah must have felt. She was extremely jealous, and in her anger she picked at Hannah continuously. Peninnah's attempt to unnerve and humiliate Hannah worked to wound and demoralize her, piercing the very core of her being. I can

imagine the subtle comments and sarcastic questions of Peninnah: "I don't know what I have done to deserve such favor from
God. I wonder why God is not blessing you with children for
Elkanah. Do you think maybe God recognizes me as Elkanah's
'real' wife? The day will come when you will lose your beauty
and charm—then Elkanah will recognize all that he holds with
me. I doubt he will have much to do with you then!"

Overwhelmed in Spirit

Each year Elkanah and his family traveled from their home
to sacrifice to the Lord at Shiloh. Whenever that day came,
he gave Peninnah and their children portions of the sacrificial
meat to eat. To Hannah, Elkanah always gave a double portion,
because he loved her.

Elkanah's attempt to show tender affection toward Hannah
only embarrassed and grieved her, because it was on those occasions that Peninnah harassed and mocked her the most. Every
year this happened. Whenever Hannah would go up to sacrifice
to the Lord, Peninnah would provoke her until Hannah was so
overcome with weeping that she could not even eat.

The special times this family set aside for joyful worship were
always interrupted by confusion, quarrels and hurt feelings.
Even Elkanah would become offended because he would take
Hannah's unhappiness personally. He just did not understand
how Hannah could get so upset about being barren when she
had him to love. He was offended by her lack of contentment.
The truth was, nobody really understood her pain—no one
except God!

"So Hannah rose after they had eaten and drunk in Shiloh.
Now Eli the priest was sitting on his seat beside a post of
the temple [tent] of the Lord. And [Hannah] was in distress

of soul, praying to the Lord and weeping bitterly" (1 Samuel 1:9–10).

In prayer Hannah asked God to look upon her afflicted soul, show mercy to her heart's cry and give her a son. There, while Hannah poured out her petition, she made a promise to God. If He would give Hannah what her heart desired, then she would give her son back to the Lord to serve Him all the days of his life. Hannah prayed fervently and wept bitterly, rapidly moving her lips yet speaking no audible words.

While Hannah prayed, Eli the priest sat at a distance observing her. Obviously he was not accustomed to such passion before God, for he perceived that she was drunk. He approached Hannah and scolded her, telling her to put away her wine!

"Hannah answered, No, my lord, I am a woman of a sorrowful spirit. I have drunk neither wine nor strong drink, but I was pouring out my soul before the Lord. Regard not your handmaid as a wicked woman; for out of my great complaint and bitter provocation I have been speaking" (1 Samuel 1:15–16).

Faith for the Impossible

When Eli realized that her soul had been crying out to God and that she had faith for the impossible, he told Hannah to go in peace. Eli assured Hannah that the Lord would answer her prayer.

Hannah believed the word of the Lord coming through her priest, and she promptly left the temple area to join her family in eating their portions of meat. Her countenance was no longer sad because faith had suddenly risen in her heart! Because of faith, Hannah *knew* the Lord had answered her prayer.

The day Hannah became desperate with God and would not let up in prayer is the day He answered her! That day Hannah became a fervent seeker and a passionate pursuer of the Lord. Her passion to see God break forth in her life motivated her in both fasting and prayer. Then her heart's cry to bear a child changed in its desire. Her delight would not only come from nurturing and loving this little child but also by blessing God and His purposes through this child. Now out of her own life many would receive ministry from God.

> Then shall your light break forth like the morning, and your healing (your restoration and the power of a new life) shall spring forth speedily; your righteousness (your rightness, your justice, and your right relationship with God) shall go before you [conducting you to peace and prosperity], and the glory of the Lord shall be your rear guard. Then you shall call, and the Lord will answer; you shall cry, and He will say, Here I am.
>
> Isaiah 58:8–9

In Hannah's time of desperation, she did not worry about what she looked like, nor did she give thought to what other people might think. Hannah could not and would not settle for less than the desire God had put in her heart the day He formed her in her mother's womb. When we passionately pursue God, we will find Him—and in finding Him, we will find His will for our lives every time! The desires we hold in our hearts will change in purpose, shaping and forming to the purposes of God. The Lord wanted Hannah to be so caught up in her pursuit of God that she would catch His heart, His vision and His will.

From Barrenness to Fruitfulness

My daughter, Jennifer, has learned some of the difficult lessons God taught Hannah. Out of her experience of being barren for nine years, and the complications and heartache that accompanied that experience, Jennifer now ministers a powerful word titled "From Barrenness to Fruitfulness."

Jennifer tells the story of her struggle with barrenness and how she also lived for some time with other incurable physical problems that caused pain and fatigue. Because she was not able to live the life she thought she would live, her disappointments began to form into negative thoughts, producing a negative spirit within her. Then out of her heart she began speaking negative words over her life.

Proverbs 18:21 says, "Death and life are in the power of the tongue, and they who indulge in it shall eat the fruit of it [for death or life]." Because of the words of her mouth and the attitudes of her heart, Jennifer found herself in a more serious state than just physical barrenness. Soon she recognized that her spirit was barren as well. Jennifer's husband would not give place to despair, nor would he settle for less than God's purpose for their lives; and after a while his tenacious faith rubbed off on her. She also rose up against the lies of the enemy and began crying out to God, asking Him to revitalize her life. Her discouragement and disappointments faded, and expectation filled her heart concerning God's intent for her life—whatever that might be.

Before long, Jennifer was transformed by the renewing of her mind in Christ and found breakthrough from barrenness, both spiritually and physically. You see, God has chosen and called each one of us to Himself, and in choosing us He calls us to fruitfulness!

"You have not chosen Me, but I have chosen you and I have appointed you [I have planted you], that you might go and bear fruit and keep on bearing, and that your fruit may be lasting [that it may remain, abide], so that whatever you ask the Father in My name [as presenting all that I AM], He may give it to you" (John 15:16).

Today Jennifer's passion is hot for God! Her heart's cry before God has changed from her own desire for natural pregnancy to God's desire and heart cry for souls not yet birthed into new life in Him (spiritual pregnancy). The product of her zeal and faith, however, also has culminated in natural life, giving us our first grandchild, Zachary Samuel. He is a miracle and a constant reminder of God's faithfulness! I know that God is using Jennifer's life and testimony to reproduce this passion in others and to impart the same tenacious faith that was imparted to her.

Testing Produces Strength

The testing and trying of Jennifer's faith was quite painful and difficult for her at times, as well as for us, her parents, to watch. Yet through those years of testing I watched as she developed and grew in wisdom, understanding and character. In both natural and spiritual aspects, the most difficult and painful times of developing and stretching have produced the greatest gifts and strengths in her life.

Our development in the Kingdom of God is much the same way. When we are born into the Kingdom, God begins to reveal to us His purposes, as well as what He has called us to do. With that, He firmly develops and strengthens the potential He placed within us while we were still being formed in our mothers' wombs.

"Your eyes saw my unformed substance, and in Your book all the days [of my life] were written before ever they took shape, when as yet there was none of them" (Psalm 139:16).

Just as Hannah had to endure the "warfare" of Peninnah, so we must face the spiritual warfare against God's purposes. In the same way God uses people to minister to us, Satan often uses people to hurt, hinder and discourage us. The devil reminds us of what we lack, encourages self-pity and speaks words that mock our hope and expectation in God. He speaks hopelessness over our lives, and to the degree we listen, to that degree we falter in faith and begin to believe it! Jennifer's pain, like Hannah's, was real, but she knew it could not be healed unless God touched that spot in her life.

Wear Faith!

Deep within our spirits God has put a holy desire to birth everything He has called us to do—both physically and spiritually. But we must keep our hearts soft and pliable before Him. We must speak life over our lives and over the purpose of our existence. It does not matter how many times we quietly hear God's voice declare His plans for our lives: If we do not pray, put our hope in Him and believe His promises, then we will die having never seen God's will performed through us. The devil continually tries to steal our joy and destroy our hope, but his efforts are powerless if we walk in faith.

"For we walk by faith [we regulate our lives and conduct ourselves by our conviction or belief respecting man's relationship to God and divine things, with trust and holy fervor; thus we walk] not by sight or appearance" (2 Corinthians 5:7).

Jennifer asks, "What do you see that God has for your life? What do you know that God is saying you can have that you don't see exist yet? Gifts? Calling? A husband? Babies? Pull on God! Hold fast! Don't let go! Declare that God is good—no matter what. We must keep our hearts soft and pliable before God. Trust Him. Don't wear self-pity—wear faith!"

That's Easy for You to Say!

The trying and testing of our faith purifies our hearts and lives. In fact, Peter said we should be exceedingly glad when we are tested because this is when the genuineness of our faith is proven. He said that the passing of these tests would redound to our praise, glory and honor when Jesus Christ is revealed (see 1 Peter 1:6–7).

When someone tries to cheer us in a trial by quoting this Scripture, however, it can sound quite irritating and the person can appear self-righteous. We might think, "That's easy for them to say—they aren't walking in my shoes!" To suggest rejoicing in difficulty might cause one to feel that God expects too much from him. Yet Peter did not write those words to a people going through mere difficulty and disappointment; he wrote them to a Church under severe persecution, imprisonment and martyrdom!

Focusing on our disappointments, pain or opposition rather than on God and His purposes for our lives always distracts us from the vision He has put within our spirits. It is during those times of distraction that we are easily beset by our human weaknesses and sins. Hebrews 12:1–2, however, tells us that we can seize our destinies or fulfill our goal in Christ if we keep our eyes upon Him. If we do, we will see what God is able to do through those very trials. When we humble ourselves before Him and cry out for His help, God will strengthen us with His ability to produce through us what seemed impossible!

Answered Prayer Turns into Daily Offering

Romans 12:12 tells us to "rejoice and exult in hope; be steadfast and patient in suffering and tribulation; be constant in prayer." And God answered Hannah's faithfulness. In due time she bore a son and named him Samuel, which means "heard of God." She named him Samuel because she said, "I have asked him of the Lord" (1 Samuel 1:20).

> And Elkanah and all his house went up to offer to the Lord the yearly sacrifice and pay his vow. But Hannah did not go, for she said to her husband, I will not go until the child is weaned, and then I will bring him, that he may appear before the Lord and remain there as long as he lives. Elkanah her husband said to her, Do what seems best to you. Wait until you have weaned him; only may the Lord establish His word. So Hannah remained and nursed her son until she weaned him.
>
> 1 Samuel 1:21–23

After Samuel was weaned and presented to the Lord, he remained in Shiloh for the rest of his life. There he was raised, mentored and trained to be one of God's greatest prophets. He was also the last prophet who ruled Israel as a judge. So powerful was the anointing upon his life that the Scriptures tell us none of his words fell to the ground (see 1 Samuel 3:19)!

It is interesting to note that Scripture tells us year after year Elkanah took his family with him and offered the sacrifice to pay his vow. After Samuel was weaned, however, Hannah took her son with her and offered her own sacrifice to pay *her* vow. Hannah no longer received only divided portions from her husband's ministry to God, but now she also gave her own offering to the Lord. Even though Hannah offered the required sacrifice of a three-year-old bull, an ephah of flour and a skin bottle of wine to pour over the burnt offering, her son Samuel became Hannah's real gift and sacrifice to God. A true and complete sacrifice is one that personally costs something. Hannah's sacrifice was not just an offering given once a year; hers was a daily sacrifice of living without her son by her side.

A Triumphant Spirit

In the past I imagined Hannah's heart breaking. She had made a vow before God in a moment of distress and because of it was required to keep her vow! I could never understand how Hannah could release her small child for someone else to train and raise. I thought surely God would consider the state of mind she was in as she sought Him for a child. Surely it would have been okay to have a discussion with God concerning the old, unreasonable promise she had made to Him. Could she not—and should she not—have asked for more time to nurture Samuel before releasing him for training? I thought God would certainly agree that eighteen was a much better age to send him to seminary.

Yet Hannah did not renege on her promise to God. And, further, her heart was not sorrowful concerning it. Instead the Word tells us that her heart exulted in triumph! "Hannah prayed, and said, My heart exults and triumphs in the Lord; my horn (my strength) is lifted up in the Lord. My mouth is no longer silent, for it is opened wide over my enemies, because I rejoice in Your salvation" (1 Samuel 2:1). Hannah's heart delighted, rejoiced, celebrated and boasted in God's victory and success. Confusion and humiliation no longer silenced her, but now she joyfully proclaimed God's goodness, faithfulness and salvation to others—a lot!

Hannah praised God:

There is none holy like the Lord, there is none besides You; there is no Rock like our God. Talk no more so very proudly;

101

let not arrogance go forth from your mouth, for the Lord is a God of knowledge, and by Him actions are weighed. The bows of the mighty are broken, and those who stumbled are girded with strength. Those who were full have hired themselves out for bread, but those who were hungry have ceased to hunger. The barren has borne seven, but she who has many children languishes and is forlorn. The Lord slays and makes alive; He brings down to Sheol and raises up. The Lord makes poor and makes rich; He brings low and He lifts up. He raises up the poor out of the dust, and lifts up the needy from the ash heap, to make them sit with nobles, and inherit the throne of glory. For the pillars of the earth are the Lord's, and He has set the world upon them. He will guard the feet of His godly ones, but the wicked shall be silenced and perish in darkness; for by strength shall no man prevail. The adversaries of the Lord shall be broken to pieces; against them will He thunder in heaven. The Lord will judge [all peoples] to the ends of the earth; and He will give strength to His king (King) and exalt the power of His anointed (Anointed His Christ).

1 Samuel 2:2–10

With our human reasoning, we cannot understand the heart and will of God; but when we have a passion for Him, the eyes of our understanding are opened to glimpse His glorious, eternal purposes. God will lift us up to see from His perspective, and seeing will change our hearts and minds toward His will!

Breaking through adversity into God's intentions for one's life always produces a triumphant spirit within us, and out of what once was barren comes forth much fruit! Hannah had given her all to God. Hers became a life of sacrifice, and out of her sacrifice came the word of the Lord to people, to kings and to nations. "Now the boy Samuel grew and was in favor both with the Lord and with men. . . . The Lord was with him and let none of his words fall to the ground" (1 Samuel 2:26; 3:19).

God Is Waiting for Us to Give Him Our All

Pregnancy causes change and usually some discomfort and great pain. Even though this discomfort and pain is a known fact, women want to be pregnant, to be filled with that new life. Pregnancy and giving birth are natural desires God has deposited into women, and barren women weep and mourn over the emptiness they feel and over their unfulfilled desire to reproduce. A woman cannot reproduce if she is barren.

It is the same in the spiritual realm. Spiritually speaking, many women have become barren. Spiritual barrenness is not always due to physical barrenness, but perhaps to other obstacles, such as wounds, disappointments and pain, that prevent God's daughters from fulfillment. Barren women often feel unfulfilled and carry a sense of shame and rejection, and this has the potential to lead to bitterness—and most often does. Hannah's natural barrenness can be likened to spiritual barrenness—the inability to birth God's gifts and the inability to reproduce the life and purposes of God in others, as well as release them to their mandate in God.

God waits for us to give our all to Him. He seeks women in His Kingdom who are like Hannah, who keep their hearts soft and pliable before Him. Like Hannah, we must walk in faith, praying, hoping in Him and believing His promises. And then when He answers our prayers and gives us the desire of our hearts concerning His will, we must be faithful to His plan and purposes. If we live like Hannah, then we cannot help but reproduce what He accomplishes in us. If we do not live like Hannah, then we may die never having seen God's will performed through us.

Are you willing to give your life as a living sacrifice to the Lord? If you are, then God can use you as a mother in His Kingdom to fulfill His purposes on this earth. If you are, then you will prove for yourself what is the good and acceptable and perfect will of God (see Romans 12:1–2). If you are, then out of your life God will produce and perform great and mighty things!

> Now to Him Who, by (in consequence of) the [action of His] power that is at work within us, is able to [carry out His purpose and] do superabundantly, far over and above all that we [dare] ask or think [infinitely beyond our highest prayers, desires, thoughts, hopes or dreams]—To Him be glory in the church and in Christ Jesus throughout all generations forever and ever. Amen (so be it).
>
> Ephesians 3:20–21

7

THE KIND OF PRAYER
THAT CHANGES THINGS!

THE PHONE RANG one midweek morning in 1982 while I was busy doing our family's laundry. I answered and was alarmed to hear my friend Diana weeping at the other end of the line.

"Shirley, can you talk? I don't know what to do!"

Never had I known Diana to be so upset. I was sure something horrible had happened since I had seen her a few days earlier at church, when she had been her usual bubbly, joyful self. Silently I began praying for a word of wisdom. Diana loved God, and I was sure that whatever the problem was, He would meet her need.

As Diana began to unveil the source of her intense emotional state, however, I really did not know what to think. In fact, I struggled to find words to respond. You see, that morning before going to work, Diana's husband, Tim, had failed to take out the garbage as he promised he would! Apparently this scenario had taken place for several weeks, and Diana had hit one of those "I can't take it anymore!" levels.

She continued talking about their broken trash agreement, and the more she talked the more nervous I became. I knew she was waiting for me to respond, but for the life of me I could not think of one intelligent thing to say! I also knew I might offend my dear friend if I was insensitive or careless with my words. She was definitely in emotional and mental pain from her disappointment, but the truth was I really could not *feel* her pain!

In the midst of listening to her frustration about her wounded feelings, I prayed harder—but this time for grace. "Lord, this is so petty! What am I going to tell her?"

Diana was a young woman who in many ways was still discovering married life. This was nothing—or at least not a major issue. I was confident that if Tim and Diana communicated with one another about this problem, they would work through their small misunderstanding. Surely in the process they would become more sensitive, supportive and appreciative concerning their lives together.

After a period of silence that finally demanded a response, I asked if she had expressed her disappointment and hurt feelings to Tim as she had just done with me.

Diana answered, "Shirley, I have talked sweetly to him about this. I have cried and even yelled at him!"

Then in a voice of desperation she continued, "Shirley, the problem really isn't about the trash ... it really isn't! The real problem is an attitude. This attitude is affecting everything Tim does, and it is certainly affecting and hurting our relationship. Even more importantly, I see it affecting his relationship with the Lord. Nothing I've tried to do or say has been able to change things—not even prayer!"

Suddenly, with that last statement, God spoke to my heart and immediately released the word and counsel I had been praying to receive.

God simply said, *You do not have, because you do not ask. [Or] you do ask [God for them] and yet fail to receive, because you ask with wrong purpose and evil, selfish motives. Your intention is [when you get what you desire] to spend it in sensual pleasures* (James 4:2–3).

Can you imagine calling a friend for comfort and she quotes that Scripture to you? I could not help but think, "Thanks a lot, God!"

I had been worrying about offending Diana with my lack of compassion for her situation. Yet the word God spoke seemed harsh in comparison to anything I might have come up with! I searched to hear something else, but this Scripture was the only thought cogent in my mind. I knew it was God's word to her.

Fearfully, yet boldly, I spoke those words in obedience to God. Little did I realize then that I, along with Diana, was about to learn an invaluable principle. God's word for her situation would become a direct lesson to us—and with it, a key that would bring understanding and wisdom into God's wonderful ways and purposes through prayer. Since that time so many years ago, I have taught this principle or key at different gatherings. Miraculous results have always followed!

Splitting Hairs

I struggled for a few moments and then asked Diana if we could split hairs! To *split hairs* means "to make a minute distinc-

107

tion in reasoning." As Christians we do not want to lean on our own understanding, but in all our ways we want to acknowledge God so that He can direct our paths (see Proverbs 3:5–6).

I quickly agreed with Diana that God wants all of us to be faithful to our promised word and that He certainly is concerned about our attitudes. God wanted her to be happy, and He also wanted Tim's heart to be ordered right in perspective to God's will for his personal life. I believed that she was right in many of the things she said.

After hearing God speak His Word, however, I asked, "When you prayed about this particular situation, was your motive directed toward your own happiness, pleasure and comfort? In other words, were you asking God to change Tim so things would be easier and more pleasant for you?"

I asked her to examine her heart to see if there was any selfish motive in her prayer.

Then apologetically I said, "I am sorry, but this is the only thing I can think to say about your situation, and I think I have heard it from God." My honest concern at that moment was for our friendship. Before I was even able to finish speaking, however, Diana blurted, "Yes! Absolutely yes! I have been praying with a wrong motive!"

"Diana, let's speak prophetically about Tim for a while. Let's talk about the things that we know God has purposed for his life. What has God called him to do? What gifts do you see operating in his life?" I asked.

As Diana and I talked about this man whom we both love and admire, we saw him as the man of God that he is. Our conversation changed to God's intention for his life, and the whole atmosphere changed to joy and expectation for the future.

Lightheartedly I asked, "Now, Diana, what kind of a man are you married to?"

Immediately Diana responded, "The most wonderful man in the world!"

I reminded her that God had chosen her, out of all of the women in the world, to be his wife. What an honor! There was no other person in this world who could minister to his heart or meet any of his needs quite the way she could. Diana alone had the privilege of holding his hand, standing by his side and blending her life, gifts and calling with his for one purpose: the praise and glory of God!

As Diana's heart overflowed with gratefulness for the high call she had been given as Tim's wife, she began to praise and thank God. While she was in the midst of thanking Him, I said, "Now, Diana, ask the Lord to take care of those things you called about earlier."

I will never forget her words! Rejoicing in the love and will of God, Diana said, "Father, please speak to Tim's heart about these things, for they are hindering *Your* purposes."

God Answered

The very next morning the telephone rang around the same time as it had the day before. Once again Diana was crying at the other end of the line. The first thought that went through my head was, "Oh, no! I don't know what else to tell her!"

Diana quickly assured me, however, that this time the tears were not of sorrow but of joy. Excitedly she explained what had taken place during the night while she slept.

Tim had a dream in which God spoke to his heart about the very things Diana had been trying to tell him. In this dream

Tim saw a beautiful home. Everything within and outside this home was in perfect order, modeled and decorated to his explicit taste. While Tim looked through the windows of this home, he prayed, "Lord, this is what I want!"

Immediately the Lord responded, *The things you desire are My will to perform. However, you determine what you receive.*

The spiritual symbol of a house or home is often interpreted as a life or family. Tim had some long-range goals that had been imparted to his heart by God. He was also a man who was strong in faith. Tim not only believed God's word, but he also longed for and anticipated fulfilling his destiny in Christ. Yet like so many of us, he had gotten caught up in everyday life with the attitudes and frustrations that confront us. When this happens, our lives get out of order according to God's will and purpose. In that dream, God went on to tell Tim that if he wanted order to exist within his home and family, then he must lead them in that kind of order. The Lord revealed to Tim that his attitude and human reasoning were hindering the fulfillment God had for his life.

When Tim understood what the Lord was speaking to his heart, it broke him and he humbly repented to both God and Diana. Through his repentance, God empowered Tim to make changes that would move him toward God's will. What Diana had been unable to relay to Tim's heart for weeks, God relayed overnight!

Too often our prayers are hindered by the motives behind them, even though our prayers may be God's will to perform. If our focus has been on ourselves, our comfort, our own pleasure or our own satisfaction instead of on God's purposes, then we have a wrong motive!

Diana could have argued that God wanted Tim to be faithful to his commitment to take out the trash. She could have argued that

God did not want her small children to follow her toward their busy road when she had to be the one to take it out. She could have argued that the children needed to see strong leadership from their father. And she certainly could have argued that God cared about her happiness. All these things are true. But they all fit into the bigger picture of God's eternal purpose for Tim's life. Because Diana humbly received the word of the Lord without trying to justify herself, she found an immediate answer to her prayer—the answer that was God's intention from the beginning.

After Diana conveyed what had taken place in less than 24 hours, I was completely amazed! Their marriage problem had not been a serious one, nor was it something she could not have lived with. After understanding the principle of James 4:2–3, however, not only did her heart change, but her motive in prayer changed as well. Then her prayer changed *things*.

"The prayer of the upright is His delight! . . . He hears the prayer of the [consistently] righteous (the upright, in right standing with Him)" (Proverbs 15:8, 29).

God Will Teach Us the Way to Choose

"He leads the humble in what is right, and the humble He teaches His way. All the paths of the Lord are mercy and steadfast love, even truth and faithfulness are they for those who keep His covenant and His testimonies. . . . Who is the man who reverently fears and worships the Lord? Him shall He teach in the way that he should choose" (Psalm 25:9–10, 12).

Because Tim and Diana loved and feared the Lord, they humbly received what God had spoken to them both. In faithfulness to His Word, God taught them in the way they should choose. Diana chose to change her own heart rather than focus on Tim's faults. She chose to lift her eyes above her circumstance to see God's heart and will. Then she chose to pray for Tim out of the very heart of God. The results were immediate!

Tim, too, chose rightly. He chose to humble himself and repent to both Diana and God and to allow the Lord to make changes in his life. But his change might not have happened without Diana's proper motive and heart attitude. Because her prayer was rightly motivated, her prayer had the power to *change things*.

Seeing the Man Complete

The principle Diana learned regarding prayer not only transformed her prayer life, but it also taught her to see others as Christ sees them—complete in Him! The revelation to pray out of a passion for God's purposes rather than her own happiness became embedded in Diana's spirit. Shortly after, she wrote the following song and dedicated it to her husband.

A Man Complete

Verse 1
In the kingdom of our home
You bring the riches of peace and joy.
We celebrate our being one
With love, music and laughter.

Chorus:
You are my David
Because you are my king.
You are my Abraham
Because you are my lord.
And like Joseph you bring me your dreams.
In the *Lord* you're a man complete!

112

Verse 2
As a servant in your tents
I see a faith so strong and true,
And I can go along with you
To discover God's ways and live. *Repeat Chorus*

Verse 3
As God reveals to you His plan
And you walk in righteousness,
It will give the Father glory
And bring His blessing to the land. *Repeat Chorus*

Diana Thomas, April 1982

Some time later at a local fair, the couple sang songs written by Tim. Suddenly Diana looked into her husband's eyes and began to sing her song, "A Man Complete." All around, men stopped to listen. Clearly the looks on their faces reflected their desire for someone to see beyond their faults, weaknesses and struggles and to recognize the potential within them.

Lifting our eyes in prayer to see God's perfect will and intention is prophetic prayer uttered in faith. No wonder so much power is released! God always watches over His Word to perform it!

Could This Be a Key?

I had been so impressed by the speedy answer to Diana's prayer that I could not help but consider the millions of other Christian women who are frustrated and discouraged. Many are either married to an unbeliever or to a Christian man who will not lead his family in the ways of God.

I questioned, "Could it be that God has just shown us a key that will answer prayer of this sort and bring the changes these women long for and have been praying for?" I wondered about women who have won their unbelieving husbands to God or their believing husbands to the ways of the Lord simply by their behavior and chaste conduct (see 1 Peter 3:1–2). Could they have accomplished such a great feat because they love God so much that their true desire is for His Kingdom to come and His will to be done on earth as it is in heaven?

This kind of passion for God and His purposes causes a woman to forget herself and enables her to capture the heart of God for mankind. The woman who wins her husband is a woman who knows and understands true love. She is able not only to love God but also to love her husband the way the Lord loves him, therefore praying perfectly and effectively. She is not afraid to lose her life because she understands God's promise that when she does, she will find it.

First Peter 3:1–2 says:

In like manner, you married women, be submissive to your own husbands [subordinate yourselves as being secondary to and dependent on them, and adapt yourselves to them], so that even if any do not obey the Word [of God], they may be won over not by discussion but by the [godly] lives of their wives, When they observe the pure and modest way in which you conduct yourselves, together with your reverence [for your husband; you are to feel for him all that reverence includes: to respect, defer to, revere him—to honor, esteem, appreciate, prize, and, in the human sense, to adore him, that is, to admire, praise, be devoted to, deeply love, and enjoy your husband].

You might wonder, *Could a woman really subordinate herself in such a manner and honestly respect herself?*

Absolutely! Because she trusts God's faithfulness and obeys His voice, she has the fire of God burning within her. The Christian woman described by Peter is not anxious or overwrought but walks in perfect peace, confidence and power. She has not become a doormat for her husband but rather a pathway leading him toward the entrance of eternal life through Christ Jesus. Because she is filled with the joy of the Lord, her presence lights up his life! "The light in the eyes [of him whose heart is joyful] rejoices the heart of others" (Proverbs 15:30). Her peaceful and joyful conduct not only enables her to win her husband to God, but it also enables her husband to fall head over heels more in love with her than he ever could imagine!

Putting the Key to the Test

Of course, the principle of God found in James 4:2–3 is a principle of prayer not only for the marriage relationship. Rather, it is a principle regarding the issues of our own hearts when in prayer for any matter. In fact, until that morning in 1982 I had only considered that portion of Scripture as referring to prayer for things, not prayer involving relationships. That day, however, I learned a powerful lesson regarding prayer for my loved ones, my own self and the world around me.

Shortly after Diana's experience, I decided to teach on James 4:2–3 at a gathering for married women. I planned not to share Tim and Diana's story. Tim was not a bad guy! I wanted to protect his reputation from his temporary insensitivity, and besides, I still thought the trash incident was a small and insignificant crisis. I was afraid women with real marital problems might become irritated by it and completely ignore the principle being taught. When I completed my talk, however, and asked if there were any questions, Diana volunteered their story, and to my surprise, just the opposite took place.

A woman I hardly knew (I will call her Lauren) asked for prayer. She told us that her husband was in the Army and was stationed in another state. Since Lauren did not like military life and because he was not a Christian, she decided to live with her mother until he was released from the military. She only saw her husband when he had a leave of absence.

That very day Lauren had received a phone call requesting that she fly down to meet him. Because he was about to be released from the military, he wanted to discuss getting a divorce so he could go on with his life.

Lauren cried while she spoke, and I could not help but notice that she was very pregnant! She told us that she had been praying for her husband's salvation but now realized her real motive and focus had been on her own happiness. Weeping, Lauren told us that she did not want a divorce. She asked us to pray that God would change her husband's mind, save his soul and redeem their marriage.

I told Lauren that God loved her husband more than she ever could, and I asked her to picture him complete in Christ. Even though he was not a believer, it was God's intention that he come to know and love the Lord! "What kind of man do you think your husband would be if Jesus was Lord of his life?" I asked.

After thinking for a few moments, Lauren began describing to us what she thought he would be like, and just as it had been with Diana, gratefulness, faith and expectation rose up within her. Smiling, she said, "Surrendered and yielded to God? Well, he would be the most wonderful man in the world!"

After reminding Lauren of her high call to intercede for his salvation, I encouraged her to thank God for his life. While praying, she repented of her wrong attitudes and also for refusing to live with him while he was in the military. Lauren's heart longed to see and love her husband again, and at the same time it was breaking over what seemed impossible. She prayed that it would not be too late! Then we all agreed in prayer for her husband's salvation, as well as for the restoration of their marriage.

It was a couple of weeks before I saw Lauren again. I remember the first thing I noticed, though. It was her beautiful, radiant smile. With a sound of wonder in her voice she said, "He does not want a divorce, and he will be home in two weeks!"

Within three weeks of arriving home, this young man was saved, baptized in water and the Holy Spirit and functioning within their local church. Lauren had not seen answers to her prayers regarding her husband for three years; but after changing her attitude and motive she found immediate breakthrough and the answer for which she had been longing.

A Humble Prayer of Intercession

It is important to remember that praying this way is not a prayer of manipulation but a prayer of humility. It is a prayer of intercession on behalf of God's purposes for someone we love.

I have prayed for my own children this way. At times I have been disappointed by some of their mistakes because they chose to lean on their own understanding rather than on God's Word. I remember waking up in the middle of the night, grieving over the spiritual condition of one of my children. I was grieving, but I was also angry because this child knew better. That night I tossed and turned, and in my mental anguish I prayed and asked God to bring conviction to the heart of my child. As I prayed my stomach tightened in knots, and pressure from stress squeezed my head.

While I was praying the Lord spoke to me and said, *You can lie awake all night and make yourself sick by morning, or you can pray for your child the way you have taught women to pray for their husbands!*

I repented for my embarrassment and anger over the situation and then arose to my high calling of intercession. I thanked God for the honor and privilege of giving birth to such a fine person. I thanked Him for the plans and purposes my child was born and destined to fulfill, and then I asked God not to allow any person or demon to interfere with or to steal what God has purposed for His glory. Two days later my child called to tell me that God had answered my prayer.

I have many other stories like this one. Each has caused me to marvel at the truth of the James 4:2–3 principle. The Bible says that the "earnest (heartfelt, continued) prayer of a righteous man makes tremendous power available [dynamic in its working]" (James 5:16).

When we ask God for help and relief or we ask God to change things, our hearts must be in right standing with Him, others and ourselves. If our own minds and spirits are not in agreement, we will strive in disunity with even ourselves. If we humble ourselves, however, totally surrendering to God and aligning our hearts with His, our prayers have the power to actualize God's will on earth. Our motive and purpose in prayer has *everything* to do with receiving the answer we already know is His will.

Interceding for Righteousness' Sake

One story from the life of David teaches us a lot about a woman's calling to intercede for righteousness' sake. As a soldier David faithfully served King Saul, and because of his acts of courage he was known and favored by the king. But Saul became angry and jealous because the people of Israel loved and respected David more than they did him. So Saul sought to kill David, who fled from him. While he was hiding to save his life, four hundred men gathered with David at the cave of Adullim. "And when his brothers and all his father's house heard it, they went down there to him. And everyone in distress or in debt or discontented gathered to him, and he became a commander over them" (1 Samuel 22:1–2).

After the prophet Samuel died, David and his men went up to the wilderness of Paran. A rich man by the name of Nabal lived in the city of Maon, but his business and possessions were in Carmel, where he was shearing three thousand sheep and a thousand goats. Some of Nabal's shepherds had been with David and his men, and David had watched out for them and protected them. When David heard that Nabal was shearing his sheep in Carmel, he told ten of his men to go there and greet and bless Nabal and his household in David's name. David told his men to inform Nabal of his kindness to Nabal's shepherds, as well as the friendship that was formed when they were all together in Paran. David's men had not taken anything from Nabal's shepherds while they were together, but now David and his men were in need. He instructed them to say, "Therefore let my young men find favor in your sight, for we come at an opportune time. I pray you, give whatever you have at hand to your servants and to your son David" (1 Samuel 25:8).

David's name was famous throughout that region. He was a warrior and well known for his many exploits. Of course, David was expecting a friendly and neighborly exchange. But Nabal was rough and evil in his ways, and he operated his business affairs with neither courtesy nor integrity. Even though Nabal's shepherds confirmed what David's men said, Nabal refused to give them food or to help them in any way, saying he did not believe them.

When David heard these things, he was irate! He and his men had helped meet every need Nabal's servants had when they were together. They had truly cared for them and even fought to protect them. Yet when David and his men were in need, Nabal's answer was crude and harsh and he treated them as enemies. David was an upright man who loved truth and righteousness, and this was just downright wrong! He could not and would not tolerate Nabal's rude treatment. Nabal's ungrateful and selfish greed infuriated David so much that he ordered four hundred men to mount their horses and quickly ride with him to destroy Nabal and everything he had.

In the meantime one of Nabal's servants ran to inform his wife, Abigail, of what her husband had done. Though Nabal was a wicked man, his wife was not. She was a sweetheart who was beautiful, both inside and out. She treated her servants with fairness and kindness and was a woman of good understanding (see 1 Samuel 25:3). Nabal's servant told Abigail how David had shown kindness to them and how his men had protected them. He said, "David's men were very good to us, and we were not harmed, nor did we miss anything as long as we went with them, when we were in the fields. They were a wall to us night and day, all the time we were with them keeping the sheep" (1 Samuel 25:15–16). The servant told Abigail that while they were away in Carmel, they never missed any of their belongings as long as David's men were with them. Then the servant asked Abigail to consider what she should do. Nabal was such a wicked man that no one could speak to him, and now because of him evil was determined not only against Nabal but his entire household as well (see 1 Samuel 25:17).

Make Haste to Intercede

First Samuel 25:18 says, "Abigail made haste"! Quickly she took two hundred loaves, two skins of wine, five sheep already dressed, five measures of parched grain, one hundred clusters of raisins and two hundred cakes of figs and laid them on donkeys. She told her servants to immediately take them to David and his men and she would soon follow.

After riding toward Paran to find David, Abigail finally saw him. Immediately she jumped off her donkey and fell quickly to her face before him to show him honor and respect!

While kneeling at his feet she said, "Upon me alone let this guilt be, my lord. And let your handmaid, I pray you, speak in your presence, and hear the words of your handmaid" (1 Samuel 25:24).

Holding still in intercession, Abigail waited for her release to speak more. When it was granted, she asked David not to be upset by the foolish and wicked thing her husband had done. She explained that this was just how he was. She told David that her husband's name even meant wicked and foolish! Even though this might sound disrespectful to some, in actuality she was interceding for his life and the lives of their household. Then she added that if she had known they were in need she would have graciously returned kindness back to them.

"So now, my lord, as the Lord lives and as your soul lives, seeing that the Lord has prevented you from bloodguiltiness and from avenging yourself with your own hand, now let your enemies and those who seek to do evil to my lord be as Nabal" (1 Samuel 25:26).

Abigail not only interceded for her household but also for David, saying, "When the Lord has done to my lord according to all the good that He has promised concerning you and has made you ruler over Israel, This shall be no staggering grief to you or cause for pangs of conscience to my lord, either that you have shed blood without cause or that my lord has avenged himself. And when the Lord has dealt well with my lord, then [earnestly] remember your handmaid" (1 Samuel 25:30–31).

David blessed the Lord for sending Abigail to him. He blessed her discretion, he blessed her advice and he blessed Abigail for keeping him from blood guiltiness and avenging himself with his own hands. David accepted what she had brought him and sent her home. Because Nabal was drunk when she arrived, however, Abigail waited until morning to tell him the things that had happened. When Nabal realized what had taken place, his heart failed him and he died about ten days later. When David heard that Nabal was dead, he earnestly remembered Abigail, just as she had requested, and he sent for her to become his wife (see 1 Samuel 25:32–42).

Many women are married to selfish and unrighteous men who, because of unjust dealings in business and relationships, jeopardize the welfare and peace of their entire families. Abigail's example, however, proves that God will honor and vindicate those who are diligent in righteousness. Even though Nabal was the head of his home, Abigail made haste to stand in the gap and through intercession cover every member of her household. Although she had done nothing wrong, Abigail identified with her husband's sins and asked that his guilt be transferred to her and then forgiven.

Abigail made haste to bow before the soon-coming king and to intercede for her household. Because of this, God saved them from destruction, removed the wicked one from them and exalted her to royalty! If she had not been diligent in righteousness, they might not have known such a great salvation!

Training Women to Pray

Abigail is an example for all spiritual mothers. We should strive not only to be like Abigail, but also to train others to be like her. If the older women will train their spiritual daughters in the act of intercession, teaching them to love righteousness, deny selfish ambitions and keep the motives of their hearts pure, an entire army of holy and dedicated women will arise to minister effectively in these end times. Whether single or married, this troop of women will bless the Father's agenda to establish His Kingdom in the hearts of mankind. Their beautiful passion for truth and justice will motivate them to take action, rather than striking out in anger, cowering or being silenced by fear. Instead they will praise and pray to the One who is their Deliverer, Christ Jesus their King. Out of their mouths will spring forth godly counsel to save and help others. Truly, those like King David whom God anoints to rule will bless the Lord for the intercession of God's powerful women!

Holy Father

Holy Father, Precious Jesus, Spirit of the Living God,
You are speaking, we are hearing, give us ears to comprehend.

123

All self-seeking, human reasoning, all our wisdom we lay
down,
That we may know You by Your Spirit, reveal to us Your
Kingly crown!

Chorus
Until all the earth bows at Your feet, 'til You finally are
crowned
King of kings and Lord of lords over all, we will pray Your
glory down!
'Til Your throne's established in the earth, 'til You reign in
majesty,
As Your will is done in heaven, Lord, let Your will be done in
me!

Bridge
And when Your Kingdom comes to earth, Your vanquished
foes brought down,
Only then will we be satisfied to lay this burden down!

Copyright 1997 Timothy Alan Thomas

8

Teamwork
with Husbands

I N THE SEVENTIES the gift of teaching was revived and activated within the Church. During that time a lot of strong teachers came forth with solid teaching, serving to help restore and establish God's people in Christian living. Suddenly teaching was available almost everywhere one looked. Local churches, Christian books, audiotapes, television and small, intimate mentoring groups ministered through the anointing of this gift. Great hunger followed after the accessible teaching, and the Church was blessed by its learning.

During that era family teaching became a major focus, and clear understanding concerning relationships with family members was once again instituted. Scriptural counsel and godly wisdom pertaining to behavior, attitudes, honor and obedience emerged for husbands, wives, parents and children. People were amazed as both spiritual and practical revelation turned into the application of sound doctrine and brought about real changes in homes. Frequently the older generation exhorted young couples, saying, "You don't know how fortunate you are to have family teaching. When we were young we did not have this knowledge or understanding, so we often suffered while having to learn the hard way!"

What the older generation said was true. We have been blessed. Family teaching has helped to mature and develop the Church toward its full strength, and it remains a foundation to build upon for ministry within the Church today. It serves as a platform and springboard for every valid ministry serving the purposes of God. And the husband/wife relationship is at the core of the family unit.

This is why I believe so strongly in husband/wife teamwork. When harmonizing together, this team exemplifies the very Godhead. When in discord, it hinders and even perverts the purposes God has for His Church. It is God's will for Christian couples to grasp together the fullness of joy, power and freedom He has ordained for them while they fulfill their specific mandate. It is only through the love and unity of blended hearts that we can accomplish anything for God. My prayer is that you might experience the completeness and satisfaction of God's blessings, found and released through the unity of such an intimate team.

Made for Each Other

Even though Adam was made in the image of God and had a loving and intimate relationship with His Creator, he longed for more. Adam's flesh cried out for companionship of another kind—one that was exactly like him. He noticed that the animals reproduced. He watched as they cuddled and slept together and then awakened, stretched and walked off together into the Garden of Eden. Yet Adam could not find another creation like him to share in a similar way. He saw no being into whose understanding eyes he could gaze or whose hand fit perfectly into his, or whose feet could walk in even stride and tempo with his own. With whom could he laugh while watching the playful animals frolic in the Garden? To whom could he talk at suppertime after a long day overseeing the new Kingdom on earth? Adam longed for another like himself to whom he could communicate his desires, but after examining every creature God had created on the earth, Adam was unable to find one that satisfied the longing of his heart.

God saw the desire of Adam's heart and the lack of fulfillment in it, and He said, "It is not good (sufficient, satisfactory) that the man should be alone; I will make him a helper meet (suitable, adapted, completing) for him" (Genesis 2:18). So God caused Adam to fall into a deep sleep, and He separated a rib from his side. From what had once been a part of Adam, God created woman. He named her Eve and presented her to Adam as a perfect and precious gift. God never intended for this gift to be neglected, unappreciated, abused or set aside as unimportant. Instead the gift of woman was given to complete man in every way. God's recorded comment right after the presentation of His gift to Adam was, "This is good!"

Isn't that wonderful? When God made woman, He made us the same as man—yet different! You see, Adam was not longing for a clone; he was longing for a companion.

God had created man in His own image out of His own love and desire for fellowship. So He understood Adam's longings!

127

Because God found such pleasure in and through His creation, He wanted Adam to know this pleasure as well. God knew the greatest companion for Adam could only be birthed out of Adam's very being, which held his passionate need. In a sense God separated Adam from himself and purposefully remade him to be unfinished and handicapped. Then, out of what had been separated, God formed Eve. Since she was made by what had been taken from Adam, he would consider himself incomplete unless his heart cleaved to her. United together, they would experience the power of the love that had begotten them both. Only their love could make them one again, and together both lives would experience the completeness found through their unity of body, soul and spirit.

Through the expression of their deep love for each other, God also enabled man and woman to procreate. God wanted His children to know and experience the exuberant joy of looking at the product of their love and saying along with Him, "This is good!"

Becoming Man and Wife

Genesis 2:24 and Matthew 19:5 tell us that when a man and woman get married they *become* one flesh. The word *become* tells us that a change and transformation occurs. This change begins in their hearts as they stop functioning apart from one another. Their former individual mentalities shift gear to higher performance and greater strength as they start thinking on a "we" and "us" basis. Preferring and serving one another in both thought and action produce the necessary fuel for greater achievement. In the same manner that one would blend two different ingredients together into something unique and tasty, the Lord takes two people who are different from one another and blends their lives together. As they walk in agreement, they complement and enlarge one another for the purpose to which God has called them. Their lives become enriched in the palatable kindness of God. They taste and see the goodness of the Lord together, and through their unity others benefit and experience it as well!

As the church is subject to Christ, so let wives also be subject in everything to their husbands. Husbands, love your wives, as Christ loved the church and gave Himself up for her, So that He might sanctify her, having cleansed her by the washing of water with the Word, That He might present the church to Himself in glorious splendor, without spot or wrinkle or any such things [that she might be holy and faultless]. Even so husbands should love their wives as [being in a sense] their own bodies. He who loves his own wife loves himself. For no man ever hated his own flesh, but nourishes and carefully protects and cherishes it, as Christ does the church, Because we are members (parts) of His body. For this reason a man shall leave his father and his mother and shall be joined to his wife, and the two shall become one flesh. This mystery is very great, but I speak concerning [the relation of] Christ and the church.

Ephesians 5:24–32

Becoming a Beautiful Complement

When God made man and woman in His image, He also placed within them free will. It is by choice, therefore, that wives *become* a beautiful complement to their husbands. Even by choice, this is not always easy. It takes learning, time and effort.

When God created Eve He made her a separate individual, yet one who would be connected to Adam's soul for as long as

129

they both would live. God's purpose was that Eve personally *become* suitable for Adam and that she *become* his teammate. It would only be through Eve's willful endeavor of adapting herself to Adam that she would find her completeness and fulfillment. The significance, as well as the results, of her completeness would become both a satisfaction and a complement to Adam. As ordained by their Creator, they would find joy and fulfillment in *their* identity and together fill the earth with His glory!

As wives, we have a specialty to perform through our expressions of love for the mates with whom God has joined us. Each woman's specialty is unique, for it is to function as a uniquely made helper for a one-of-a-kind man.

I truly love my husband, and I love having *become* his wife. I have come to know and understand him. He is the love of my life! Becoming one flesh with Jim is a process that has made me who I am today.

After several years of "wife-ing," I remember a temporary, vain thought I had concerning my ability and productivity as a wife. I thought, "Hey, I am pretty good at this! I know how to do this wife stuff." God interrupted my thought abruptly, however, with one single word: *Adapt!* To *adapt* means "to conform and adjust oneself to meet a need." When a woman adapts to her husband, she does far more than just accept or tolerate his uniqueness. Instead she conforms and connects herself to his life in such a way that she lays aside her self-will to connect and become a part of his. When I heard God speak, I remembered the years of dying to self and learning to adapt to my husband, which I knew must continue if I wanted my marriage to further develop and grow. I realized that if the Lord should call my husband home before me and I remarried, I would *not* be good at this. You see, I could not be the wife of another in the same way I have been to Jim. I would have to adapt myself all over again. I thought, "How awful!"

Ephesians 5:33 says, "Let the wife see that she respects and reverences her husband [that she notices him, regards him, honors him, prefers him, venerates, and esteems him; and that she defers to him, praises him, and loves and admires him exceedingly]." That is not easy to do with just any guy, you know! A woman can choose to love and respect her mate, but it still takes a lot of work to *become* the wife God calls her to be.

Losing Our Lives

"Whoever finds his [lower] life will lose it [the higher life], and whoever loses his [lower] life on My account will find it [the higher life]" (Matthew 10:39). I have quoted this Scripture since I was a child. Yet for years I did not really know its meaning and the power of the truth it holds. I only understood it to mean a form of surrender to God for our salvation. I did not understand it to include practical, everyday life. One day, however, God gave me something concrete in which to lose my life.

One afternoon as I sat quietly mending clothes, my mind began to plan for that evening. That night would entail a busy schedule for Jim, who was a youth pastor. I understood how important it was for him to spend time with the teenagers of our church, and that night after supper three teenage boys were coming over to lift weights with him in the garage. I wanted to have dinner prepared to eat the moment he came home so that he and I, along with our two small children, could sit down as a family and eat together. I had wanted some time for us to be alone, to visit and to play together before Jim was ripped away for the evening.

My responsibility and passion were for my family. Not only was my happiness found there but also my fulfillment. As I sat mending, my thoughts drifted from what I would prepare for dinner to playtime on the floor with the kids, and then finally to more personal and intimate time with just the two of us after the boys went home and the children were in bed.

Suddenly God spoke to my spirit and said, *I have called you to more!* Those words terrified and shook me, because for some reason I understood those short, few words to mean more than taking care of my husband, children and home.

With a sense of panic I replied that there was not room for more. You see, I had devoured a lot of family teaching and had made it a habit to practice the things I was learning. I was conscientiously giving myself to loving my husband and serving his needs and the needs of my children. Furthermore, I was good at what I was doing! I thought I was fully abiding in God's purpose for my life. Yet even though I felt safeguarded and confident within my home, outside of my four walls my life was a complete mess of insecurity! As God spoke those words to me, my heart was gripped by this truth.

After I cried a few "Yeah, but Lord . . ." reasons why there was not room in my life for anything besides taking care of my husband, children and home, I asked God this question: "How could I possibly find time to do more with my life?"

The Lord replied, *When you lose your life in your husband, you will find it.*

My first thought was, "Heresy! This can't be God speaking to me, because that isn't what God's Word says." But because of all the family teaching I had been devouring, I recognized that it was indeed what God's Word said. I realized God's intention for my role as Jim's helper was not to just be there and say, "Good job, Jim!" or "Dinner's ready, sweetheart." Nor was it just to be his understanding friend and companion. These things were necessary and good for building a successful marriage, but they could not change the crippled, soulish areas of my personality. I had always felt incomplete and that something in my life was amiss, and now God was telling me to lose what little identity I had in my husband. That afternoon God caused me to realize that He wanted me to lose my life in everything that makes my husband who he is. Why? Simply because he is my husband!

You may be wondering, *Is Shirley encouraging women to become doormats?* Absolutely not! Rather, we as wives are called to *become* one with our husbands, and this requires losing our lives in theirs so that we *become* one in spirit with them.

Jim's life involved more than what existed in our home. He had a history and memories that I had not shared. God gave him a ministry and burdens to carry. He had pleasures aside from me. Suddenly I desired to lose my life in all those things. God wanted me not only to come alongside him in submission but also in spirit. That day God brought a change to my mentality and an attitude change to my life by challenging me to lose it!

Now I am not talking about refusing to allow our husbands to breathe on their own. There are times we all need our space. That is healthy! Becoming a burden was not God's intention in forming woman. God showed me, however, that I had been in the background trying to support Jim in his life rather than really becoming a part of it. I realize now that I could not have grown emotionally if I remained as I was. I not only would have become frustrated and bored, but I also would have become a source of frustration and boredom to Jim. God had not appointed me to be Jim's faithful servant, but his faithful wife and companion.

Many people do not understand this principle of losing your life. Our human thoughts concerning this tell us that if we do, we will lose the personality and individuality God created. But the opposite takes place! Instead, the personality and individuality that God created a woman to possess actually blossom and flourish in strength and beauty when she loses her life in that of her husband.

In obedience to what God had just revealed to my heart, I began to lose my life in Jim. I adapted to his loves and passions by making them my loves and passions. In the same way that we both loved and nurtured our marriage and family, I began to love and nurture everything else that held Jim's heart. What took place in me over the next three weeks was nothing short of a miracle! Insecurities and inferior feelings and behavior suddenly dropped from my life. I was not looking for this to happen, nor did I make a conscientious effort to overcome my various hang-ups and fears. But when I purposed to lose my life, I truly began to operate as a team with my husband, and in that position I found freedom in peace, joy and security. We became youth pastors, and while he gave of his life to establish young disciples of Christ, I became fully involved—not only in hospitality, but also in discipling young women to follow after God. Our lives became a picture of the unity to which Christ is calling each one of us.

It is a matter of will. Are we willing to obey God's Word to us? Will we choose to let His will operate in our lives?

He tells us when we lose our lives on His account we will find them (see Matthew 10:39), regardless of our own feelings. If we govern our lives by selfish desires, His will cannot be established through us. Holding onto our own will prevents His joy and peace from taking root within us, making us unable to grow in the love of the Lord. If we are living outside God's precepts, we cannot fulfill His divine purposes. God gave us His Son, Jesus, Jesus gave His life for our salvation and the Holy Spirit was given to us to teach us how to walk in the ways of the Lord. Through God's example, we have been instructed to give our lives away as well—in fact, to lose them! Losing one's life in the context of the marriage relationship brings blessing and glory to the couple and allows God's will to be done through their lives.

Dying to Self

"Neither is new wine put in old wineskins; for if it is, the skins burst and are torn in pieces, and the wine is spilled and the skins are ruined. But new wine is put into fresh wineskins, and so both are preserved" (Matthew 9:17).

God wants us to be like new, fresh wineskins. And yet new wineskins come from freshly *killed* animals! This means we must learn to die daily, so that we can be used afresh each day by the Lord.

So many of God's children hear the Word of the Lord and get excited about it yet fail to walk out what it teaches. I am convinced the reason for this is because they simply love their own lives more than the purposes of God. They are refusing to die to self.

Self-preservation prevents us from grasping revelation and then from living out and carrying to others the new truths God reveals to us by His Holy Spirit. Instead such revelation is chased away by our human reasoning. We may hear God's Word, agree with it and even preach it, but if we do not die daily, we cannot experientially know it. If we govern our lives by our own wisdom with all of its human appetites controlling us, then God's wisdom

135

(the comprehensive insight into God's ways and purposes) will not even appeal to us and cannot effectively operate in our lives. We *must* die to self!

This principle was not designed by God to manipulate relationships or to gain favor, but to form Christ's character in us. When we lose our lives, we actually preserve them and His purposes in us. We must become new wineskins by losing our lives daily. When our lives are truly surrendered to God's will, the fresh presence of His Spirit can operate in us as He establishes His will through us.

Doing the Opposite of What You Feel

Sometimes I hear people say they just do not know how to lose their lives. How do you deal with your own desires or competitive feelings? My reply is simply to do the opposite of what you feel! Feelings get caught up in vanity, seeking attention, tolerating jealousy and other characteristics not belonging to Christ. That is when we need to practice the opposite of those emotions. When we do so, we die to self and Christ shines through us.

I remember a time I desperately wanted to become pregnant with my third child. Month after month went by without successfully conceiving, and frustration and disappointment grew within my heart.

At that time, my best friend also had two children. Susan was beautiful! She was from a wealthy family and was known for her exquisite taste. She had a lovely home, a beautiful car, beautiful clothes (of course, because I was her friend I borrowed them) and a beautiful family. It seemed that everything Susan did, she prospered in it. I had watched other women snub my friend because of their own insecurities and jealousy. But I loved her, and I refused to compare myself with her.

One afternoon while I was vacuuming my living room, however, the Holy Spirit dropped a word of knowledge into my spirit revealing that she was pregnant. It was as if I had been slapped! My heart filled with jealousy. This emotion was so sudden it surprised me! I was grieved and torn by guilt because of my heart's betrayal to my friend. After the initial shock I repented, but my negative feelings remained. She had not been praying for another child—I had.

I turned off the vacuum cleaner and said, "God, I have a real problem! I am jealous and I can't shake this feeling. I know You can see the ugliness of my heart. How can I be free from this?"

God simply said, *Do the opposite of what you feel.*

Obviously my feelings were not good! So I lifted my voice and began thanking God at once for blessing Susan with another child. I asked Him to richly bless the fruit of her womb, to give her a safe pregnancy and an easy delivery. From that moment on I sincerely rejoiced over her pregnancy as if it were my own.

Later I discovered God had revealed Susan's pregnancy to me before she even knew of it. It sounds like I was pretty spiritual, doesn't it? Well, I wasn't! God let me know that I did not receive that word of knowledge because I was smart or because I was spiritual, but because He wanted to reveal my heart to me so He could purify it. He wanted to teach me victorious living by the principle of dying to self, and He wanted to take me higher in Him.

By the way, God did answer my prayer. After Susan delivered a beautiful daughter, the doctor discovered another baby was in her womb. That afternoon my dear and beloved friend gave birth to twin daughters. Because I had done the opposite of what I felt nine months earlier, I could laugh while I declared this truth to her: "Yesterday we both had two children, but today you have twice as many!"

With God's help I was able to set my feelings of jealousy aside and lose my life so that His purposes in my relationship with my dear friend would be accomplished. Losing your life without letting your own desires or competitive feelings get in the way is only possible by doing the opposite of what you feel. Do not let your feelings get caught up in those things that do not belong to Christ. When you can do this, you are dying to yourself and letting Christ shine through you. This principle is vital to the kind of relationships God wants His children to have with one another, especially within the marriage relationship.

Practice What God Says

If we will heed the Word of God for our lives by doing what it says—whether or not it makes sense to us or whether or not we feel like it—we will be blessed! If we do not, His wisdom cannot become seasoned within us to transform and empower us for His purposes. We will be unable to walk in the revelation God's Spirit brings to us.

> But be doers of the Word [obey the message], and not merely listeners to it, betraying yourselves [into deception by reasoning contrary to the Truth]. For if anyone only listens to the Word without obeying it and being a doer of it, he is like a man who looks carefully at his [own] natural face in a mirror; For he thoughtfully observes himself, then goes off and

promptly forgets what he was like. But he who looks carefully into the faultless law, the [law] of liberty, and is faithful to it and perseveres in looking into it, being not a heedless listener who forgets but an active doer [who obeys], he shall be blessed in his doing (in his life of obedience).

James 1:22–25

If you are a married woman, I encourage you to lose your life in your husband. Do not be discouraged if he is not a believer. Through your demonstration of God's love, you have the power to win your unbelieving husband to the Lord. God is not requiring Christian women to lose their lives in sinful lifestyles. Quite the contrary! God simply requires women to love their husbands sincerely. After all, didn't Christ die for him? By appreciating your husband and by your chaste behavior, you can influence his heart to love God (see 1 Peter 3:1–2). Since this is true, don't you think a woman's behavior can also win a believing husband who is lazy or self-centered to the ways of God? If we will truly lose our lives and function as the helpers God has called us to be, then we will be blessed and our lives will be empowered for His purposes.

Losing One's Life Leads to Clearer Vision

Things began to change in our life as a married couple when I began to obey God and lose my life in my husband. As I look back upon the days when we were youth pastors, I see that particular time in my life as a training ground for everything God has called me to do. Of course, I was being trained while we pastored the youth, but the greatest training came as I learned to lose my life.

139

Whenever I would start pulling into myself again, the old insecurities I once had would start to resurface. But as long as I practiced losing my life, I continued to find it. In finding my life, I began to be filled with the vision God wanted me to have for His Church.

When teenage girls began to drop by my house just to "hang out," I was not always able to sit and talk. I had small children to attend and a home to manage. Instead I would say, "I have some beds to make, dishes to wash and clothes to fold. Come on along!" It was a great learning time for all of us. They would follow me through the house as I went about my business of caring for my household. During that time I learned to minister to these young girls by developing and cultivating a relationship with them. Through knowing them and sharing my own life with them, I became bold enough to talk, encourage and share with them concerning their walks with God.

I discovered that the more I gave myself to others, the more vision God imparted to my heart. More and more I began to understand and long for the consequences of His Church becoming fully mature. In my spirit I began to see the results of God's people growing up, coming to completeness of personality and recognizing their full potential in Him. When God's sons and daughters decide to walk together in perfect love, unity and divine order, blessing and power will be released to the world! I began praying for myself, as well as for all His sons and daughters. God wants us to renounce human reasoning that keeps us from His wisdom so that He can heal us from the wounds of our past and pour His faith into us.

God says His people are like sheep and He is the Shepherd who watches over us affectionately. I am so grateful for this, because like sheep we need constant supervision. Natural sheep can become *cast*, which is very serious and can lead to their death. When a sheep lies down—not a serious problem for most animals—and rolls onto its back it cannot roll back over. Its excess weight holds it down. Soon gases build up in its body, causing it to bloat, and it is unable to regain its balance. In addition, the sheep could die of hunger and thirst, or become open prey for its enemy. A cast sheep cannot live if the shepherd is not nearby to pick it up.

The weight of excess wool can symbolize burdens or pain that we as Christians need to release to God. Perhaps we need to have some things shaved from our lives so we can serve the purposes of God more effectively. This excess weight also can symbolize those sins that easily beset us. In that case the Bible tells us to strip ourselves of them (see Hebrews 12:1)!

But a sheep can become cast for good reasons as well. For God's Kingdom on earth to flourish, His purposes must be birthed within us. When we willfully and joyfully lose our lives on His account, Christ places within us vision for His will and anoints us to give birth to His purposes. Becoming impregnated with God's vision, however, might make our position difficult. Others around us might hate what we stand for and say, "My, my! That vision has made you fat and unattractive. You are a little too radical! You would be much more attractive and acceptable if you would just lose that vision." At times we may think we want to quit—but we cannot! That vision is in us. There is no way we will abort it, because we love it.

We carry that vision, nurture that vision and protect that vision through prayer, and we cannot be satisfied or content until we see the vision born. As time wears on, however, the vision might seem too heavy and hard to carry. We may want to say, "It has been here long enough; this is not fun anymore!" Often we lose patience. Yet if we try to force the vision into existence before its time, we will do a lot of damage.

I have had four children, and during each pregnancy there came a time when I said, "Okay, it is time to give birth. I have had it! Let's get this baby out—now!" Then when the time of hard labor finally came, weariness set in and from pure exhaustion I thought about giving up. Just as intensely as I might have earlier determined to get the baby out, I temporarily made up my mind to quit for the rest of the day. I have even said, "I'll finish doing this tomorrow."

This is when my team leader, Jim, encouraged me the most not to give up. Instead he exhorted me to push harder. We looked one another in the eye and agreed on the good thing God wanted to come forth from our lives together. And I decided once again to lose my life—that is, to endure the pain and exhaustion of birth labor—for the sake of God's purposes.

"And let us not lose heart and grow weary and faint in acting nobly and doing right, for in due time and at the appointed season we shall reap, if we do not loosen and relax our courage and faint" (Galatians 6:9).

Priscilla and Aquila: A Team

One couple in the New Testament presents a godly example of a husband and wife losing their lives for the higher calling of Christ Jesus. After the apostle Paul departed from Athens, Greece, where he had been spreading the Gospel, he went to Corinth. There he met a Christian Jew named Aquila. He and his wife, Priscilla, had just arrived from Italy because of an edict Claudius had issued stating that all Jews were to leave Rome. The edict had been passed because controversy among the Jews concerning Christianity had become great, so Claudius decided the best way to resolve the contention was simply to remove them from the land.

Aquila invited Paul to stay with him and Priscilla in their home. Since they were both tent makers, they could start a business together for income while they preached the Gospel in that region. From that moment on, Aquila's name is not mentioned alone but always along with that of his wife. Aquila and Priscilla were a team not only in business, but also in life and ministry.

"Two are better than one, because they have a good [more satisfying] reward for their labor; For if they fall, the one will lift up his fellow. But woe to him who is alone when he falls and has not another to lift him up! Again, if two lie together, then they have warmth; but how can one be warm alone? And though a man might prevail against him who is alone, two will withstand him. A threefold cord is not quickly broken" (Ecclesiastes 4:9–12).

Priscilla and Aquila were relational people and soon became part of Paul's ministry team. Not much longer than eighteen months after they had arrived in Corinth, Paul sailed for Syria, and Priscilla and Aquila accompanied him. There this team planted a church, which met in the home of Aquila and Priscilla. After a while Paul journeyed from that place to other lands, establishing disciples and imparting new strength to them, but he left Priscilla and Aquila behind to pastor this new work.

During that time they met a man named Apollos. Even though Apollos was a zealous teacher who taught diligently and accurately the things concerning Jesus, Scripture tells us that Priscilla and Aquila took him aside and expounded to him the way of God more definitely and accurately. Because of this, the ministry of Apollos developed and grew in authority and anointing.

Aquila and Priscilla were *one* in every aspect. Even their names were spoken together as if they were one name. They were recognized for their excellence in team hospitality, teaching, training and developing of leaders. Together they were the overseers of a church. When referred to in the Scriptures, Priscilla is usually mentioned first, which is a credit to her character and effective ability.

Priscilla is mentioned several times in the New Testament (see Acts 18:2, 18, 26; Romans 16:3; and 1 Corinthians 16:19). Contrary to what some people might say, we can see through her life that God does anoint women in the Church to preach, teach, equip and release others for ministry. Yet what stands out to me most is the example and picture she and her husband, Aquila, displayed through their lives together. They did not grow weary during times of difficulty but instead embraced a team spirit. Because of that, they were able to effectively spread Christianity among the Gentiles.

Paul called Priscilla and Aquila his fellow workers and found their company a source of encouragement and comfort. In fact, he affectionately refers to Priscilla by a nickname, Prisca, in Romans 16:3. This husband-and-wife team was loved by many because of their love and the work they accomplished together. Paul spoke for himself as well as all the churches among the Gentiles when he thanked them for risking their lives. They were a husband-and-wife team that was filled with the love of God, a passion for souls and the prayer for God's Kingdom to come and His will to be done on earth as it is in heaven.

God does not have to think about what He will do when His people unite their hearts together in His love and purposes. He has already commanded a blessing. Husband-and-wife teams are powerful!

This is not a team that comes together weekly or even daily, and then after accomplishing their goal travel separate ways like other teams. This team is united until death! They go to their private bedchamber each night carrying the burden of the Lord together. They talk and agree upon His purposes while falling asleep in one another's arms. Together they awaken to the vision and encourage one another as they unite their hearts afresh and anew each morning concerning the plan to which God has called them. They work together, serve together and love together.

Embracing Your Husband's Call and Ministry

God does not want us to remain like children. He wants our lives to be enfolded in love as we grow up in every way into Christ, the anointed One (see Ephesians 4:11–15). I do not think, therefore, that we should be able to distinguish men from their wives—other than that one is a father and one is a mother. Since Scriptures clearly tell wives to adapt to and submit to their husbands in everything, I believe a natural result of this will be to embrace a heart like his for God. As a woman truly adapts to her husband, her heart will take on his same passions. If he has a passion for intercession, her heart will be motivated in and through intercession. I once heard someone say, "But a plumber's wife is not necessarily a plumber!" I agree with that statement to a point. A good plumber's wife, however, finds great joy in her husband's accomplishments and the fulfillment his career or call in life brings to him. She is not only interested in the things that he does, but she also probably knows what each tool is used for and promotes and praises his work as if it were her own.

Our associate pastor, Bill Beery, oversees the prayer ministry of our church. Bill is also a prophet who has spent hours in the

Word and the presence of God. Bill's wife, Teri, would pray, but her prayer life was not considered exceptional, only adequate. In fact, there was a time when Teri could not imagine ministering as an intercessor. She did not know what it meant to love and crave after prayer. But she does now! When Bill's passion for prayer grew, Teri adapted herself to the passion of his heart. Now they go on prayer walks and pray together at length.

Teri did not originally feel called to prophesy, but because she has adapted herself to her husband she now has his heart for the prophetic ministry as well. Today they minister accurately together as a prophetic team. Teri is involved in everything Bill does, whether it is leading a cell group, marriage ministry, prayer group or prophetic ministry. She is able to assist him and to work alongside him in team ministry because she has the same heart for all these things.

Teri has chosen to adapt herself to Bill. This process has not only caused her to grow in knowledge and ability but also in influence and authority as a leader in our church. Teri has her own gifts apart from Bill, just as we all have. She is an excellent counselor and teacher of God's Word. In like manner, we have watched Bill develop and grow in Teri's gifts. You cannot separate them in ministry! When one of them speaks, the other will agree because they are one in heart, mind and spirit.

The Perfect Marriage

"Yet your desire and craving will be for your husband, and he will rule over you" (Genesis 3:16). Most women resist or at least want to ignore this Scripture. The devil is in total rebellion to God; he finds no greater pleasure, therefore, than in seeing God's children turn up their noses in resistance to their Creator's commands. Throughout the ages Satan has tried to steal our peace, joy and purpose as women—and our very identity! Since the day God verified His creation of woman as good, the devil has tried to destroy, distort and pervert the purpose for her existence. He will always try to manipulate the thoughts of mankind into viewing God's decisions as bad or at least foolish. God's idea of rulership, however, is one of benevolence and goodness.

Fulfilling our mandate as wives not only empowers and completes the "man-team," but it also brings joy to our Creator! God's purpose for the existence of Adam and Eve was that they could worship their Creator and have intimate fellowship with Him. God desired to fill the earth with His glory through the reproduction of their love for God and one another. The love and devotion we have for our mates was never meant to be a distraction from worship, but rather a satisfaction and fulfillment of our needs so that we can better focus on the love of God and our relationship with Him. The devil is terrified of the day when the Church fully awakens in love to her Creator!

And the marriage standard God gives in the example of Adam and Eve is a beautiful picture of Christ's relationship with His Church. Christ is perfecting and preparing His Bride for His eternal purposes. Her desires and cravings will be for Him. He will rule perfectly over His Bride in victory, might and protection, and together they will live and reign forever!

What an honor women have concerning their purpose and function in the creation of mankind!

THE PASTOR'S WIFE

ONE PARTICULAR GROUP of women often struggles in understanding their place within the Church as mothers in the Kingdom. These are the women who share in their husbands' call to minister.

The office of pastor inherently has a high level of stress connected with it. The pastor's responsibility is to minister to the needs of others as well as lead them in righteousness and to maturity. Some precious pastors' wives have not recognized the gifts and call upon their own lives, and many underestimate the position and valuable asset of being their husbands' helpers.

Pastors' Wives Have It Tough!

Generally speaking, it is rare to find secure women in ministry. Even the most successful women struggle with criticism and rejection, and women who are married to church leaders are no exception. In fact, leaders' wives sometimes suffer low self-esteem more than anyone else in the Church!

These women remember and are still wounded from past sheep bites inflicted upon their souls. "Baaa! Who do you think you are?" "Baaa! What kind of teaching was that?" "Baaa! You aren't properly educated!" "Baaa! Sister So-and-so does a better job than you!" "Baaa! I need your husband to pray for me. No, you can't help me. I need a minister. . . . Baaa!"

Over the last thirty years, I have talked with women in different cities, states and countries who are married to pastors. As we have confessed to one another our faults, weaknesses and burdens concerning our own lives and churches, I have found that many pastors' wives do not consider themselves to be part of their husbands' ministries. Instead they feel inadequate and inferior—especially within their own church setting. Because of this, many of these leaders' wives resist ministry of any kind.

Some pastors' wives burned out long ago. They have given up any thought of serving alongside their husbands. I cannot help but wonder, however, if their perspective was that of an unappreciated slave, rather than a servant who was a mother in the house.

Two Questions of Pastors' Wives

Jim and I minister together as a team, so I am asked from time to time about the way we function together in our church. As I share my conviction concerning women mentoring women and mothers arising in the midst of congregations, sometimes my opinion is asked about *their* place in their churches.

These are the questions most often asked:

150

1. Do you feel God expects me to minister to the women of my church?
2. If another woman is more qualified, shouldn't she be appointed to lead the women instead of me?

When asked such questions, my genuine concern is not whether or not the pastor's wife holds a ministerial position in the church, but rather for the woman herself. I usually answer with questions of my own:

1. Are you asking these questions because you do not want to minister or because you feel inadequate?
2. Does your husband want you to work alongside him in ministry? If not, why?
3. How do you feel about another woman ministering and pouring herself into the other women of the congregation—usually at least 50 percent (or more) of the congregation that your husband is overseeing?
4. Should another woman replace you in your home if she can do a better job caring for your family?

The Pastor and His Wife Must Agree

Some women adhere to caring for their husbands and raising their children as the extent of their calling in God. Yet they seem frustrated and unfulfilled in doing so! Signs of jealousy, neglect and hurt emotions—especially feeling unimportant or unneeded—begin to surface in them.

To compound the problem, the husbands of these women are often torn between feelings of guilt and failure regarding their families and ministries. These men feel they can never satisfy or reassure their wives concerning their devotion to them while still remaining faithful to their ministries. Respect for both the pastor and his wife are damaged as he realizes how heavy his burdens have become, and his joy in serving God diminishes—or even vanishes!

When this happens, the danger of bitterness taking root in the pastor's heart becomes more pressing. He silently blames himself for his lack of ability or success, and he blames his wife for not understanding or backing him in the work God has called him to do. A tired, discouraged and drained appearance often covers his countenance. If he continues in ministry without resolving these issues, his wife's feelings of displacement and insecurity, as well as disconnection from her husband's ministry, increase. Then when their children grow up and leave home, she no longer has a sense of purpose, and he feels like giving up! With their marriage relationship already weakened and strained, too often one or the other completes its destruction with an act of infidelity.

It is not my place to tell leaders' wives how God wants them to function. Jim and I hold strong views concerning husband-and-wife teamwork, and, of course, we do what God tells us to do. But we also recognize that couples must agree on the work and performance of His will for their lives together.

Recognizing the Strategies of the Devil

If a pastor and his wife do not walk in agreement, then they will be headed toward confusion and disaster regarding their own relationship with one another. These husbands and wives, therefore, must never stop sharing their hearts with one another or listening to one another's thoughts, struggles and hurts. This caring and sharing keeps the door of understanding wide open and increases their closeness. If they close the doors of their hearts, however, they are unable to live an open and transparent life with the one God designed for them to cling to.

When a woman isolates herself because her feelings are hurt, it becomes impossible for her love to develop into maturity. Instead of cultivating an understanding and gracious heart, she fosters unforgiveness, bitterness and resentment. This almost always results in a judgmental and critical spirit concerning the weaknesses of others. Most husbands find this very unattractive! If she continues this behavior through years of marriage, the tenderness he once held for his wife can be destroyed. In its place a judgmental and critical spirit can develop toward her as well. Of course, this only adds to her hurt and widens their gap.

More often than not, the relational breakdown of a couple in ministry originates from ongoing pain or frustration that the wife has experienced. Undoubtedly her privacy has been violated and her heart misunderstood at times. Although her feelings were not always wrong and her wounds are very real, if she practices isolating her heart it will destroy the intimacy the couple once shared and make their separation sure!

This vicious cycle is a deceitful strategy of Satan! His plan is to steal, kill and destroy a couple from their call, their purpose and the joy set before them by God. "The thief comes only in order to steal and kill and destroy" (John 10:10).

I believe Satan has been strategizing for centuries to discourage and hinder leaders' wives from ministering. Many women have been ripped off by the devil and held back from seeking God's will. To the degree the devil is able to wound, weaken or destroy the pastor's wife, to that degree he can wound, weaken and destroy the shepherd from leading God's flock.

No one is perfect! There are times when we become frustrated, impatient and even angry. If we yield to those fleshly emotions that try to resurrect themselves or to our human reasoning that wants to exalt itself above God's truth, our lives will eventually lead to destruction. But through God and the strength of His Spirit in us, we have power against those things. We can take wrong thinking, hurt feelings and human judgments as prisoners and command them to obey Christ! Doing this will cause us to grow in the wisdom of God and in His heart for mankind.

> For though we walk (live) in the flesh, we are not carrying on our warfare according to the flesh and using mere human weapons. For the weapons of our warfare are not physical [weapons of flesh and blood], but they are mighty before God for the overthrow and destruction of strongholds, [Inasmuch as we] refute arguments and theories and reasonings and every proud and lofty thing that sets itself up against the [true] knowledge of God; and we lead every thought and purpose away captive into the obedience of Christ (the Messiah, the Anointed One).
>
> 2 Corinthians 10:3–5

Delilah: A Woman Used by Satan

Delilah is a biblical example of how a woman can tear down her man's ministry. She allowed the enemy to use her to destroy the ministry God had given Samson.

God called Samson to serve His purposes as a judge in Israel, and He gave him strength and power to protect His people from the enemy. The angel of the Lord had instructed his parents before he was born concerning God's call upon his life, saying that a razor should never touch his hair. Samson would be a

Nazarite. His life would be consecrated to God, and in his hair would lay the secret of his strength (see Judges 13–16).

But Samson was immature in both wisdom and character. One day he fell in love with a woman named Delilah, and he set his life toward having her. Delilah's affections, however, were not set upon God but upon fleshly and material things. The enemy knew Delilah's character flaws and made her an offer her selfish ambitions could not turn down. While Samson's enemy waited to bind him powerless, Delilah exercised feminine wiles to deceive and manipulate him until he disclosed the secret and power of God concerning his strength. "When she pressed him day after day with her words and urged him, he was vexed to death. Then he told her all his mind" (Judges 16:16–17). Delilah sold his love for a sum of money and was used by his enemy to destroy him!

You may think that using Delilah as an example is an extreme illustration. I know she did not reverence or serve God, and I know Samson was hanging with the wrong crowd when he met her. Yet Delilah still had an opportunity and choice to cover herself in Samson's mantle and to help him seize his destiny in God. If they had married, she could have been a help and encouragement to Samson concerning the call and purposes of God for him. She could have influenced him to walk before God in truth and integrity. Together they could have been quite a team—Samson, mighty in deliverance, strong and steadfast against the enemy; and Delilah, tenacious in spirit, persistently pursuing what her heart desired. If she had chosen to partner with Samson concerning God's call, she would have found her destiny in Him as well.

I understand the power women have, and I sense a warning through this passage of Scripture concerning our character and behavior. We must practice and also teach women to be careful against performances such as Delilah's. We may think, "I would never turn my husband over to a bunch of thugs!" But if our hearts and motives are not pure, if our focus is on material things or on what satisfies and benefits us rather than God's Kingdom, we, too, might selfishly nag and manipulate our husband against the will of God.

The enemy of our souls lurks in the background. He waits for an opportune time to imprison and blind God's anointed ones from further vision. Using femininity to sway a husband against God's purposes and heart for mankind is not only deceitful but also can bring even the strongest man of God to destruction! We must be very careful concerning our agendas, careful what we press after and careful with our words.

Sharing Her Husband's Heart

More often than not, a pastor's wife has not considered her husband's flock as their flock together. If her mentality of training the younger women has been to oversee a program rather than to personally touch the intimate lives of people, she may have thought anyone could function in this position. But when she realizes that the Word of God requires the older woman to teach, counsel, adjust and train the younger women in both godly and natural living, then she understands that the older woman must help pastor the flock.

The pastor may have others who help lead the congregation, and he pours his heart into those who help him. In order to have the pastor's heart, then, the leading woman must spend time with him, and this is potentially dangerous if she is not his wife. God's intention is that the husband/wife team have the same heart. Working together only develops and strengthens it more! And as she begins to have the same heart as her husband, the pastor's wife can follow his example and pour that heart into the other women of the congregation, leading them as a mother in that house to become women of power.

Other women will teach and lead in the local church, but it should be with Mama's heart and under her oversight. When a leader's wife understands that ministry is not a mere job that requires time and work but is a loving, transparent relationship with those mysteriously resembling her own family, she will usually want to work alongside her husband.

Examining Our Hearts

I have met only a few women who did not have a desire to minister alongside their husbands. I have found many, however, who have the desire but feel unaccepted or uncomfortable in this position. To women who fit into the second category, I ask a couple of very important questions:

1. Does your husband's heart trust in you? If not, do you know why?
2. Does he respect your counsel? If not, do you know why?

The pastor's wife must examine her heart and life to see if there is any reason her husband might be afraid to trust her or to bring her alongside him in ministry. Our husbands know more about us than anyone else does. They live with us! They see our attitudes and hear our murmurings. They know our degree of hunger for and intimacy with God. If your husband does not know these things, then you have your answer already!

In your marriage and in your home, do you live an open and honest life? Do you practice humility? Are you quick to repent and quick to forgive? When dealing with offenses, do you listen to your husband's heart and then respond reasonably? Or do you demand your way and stubbornly push what you want?

A pastor is responsible to watch out for the welfare of his flock. Do you love the people in your church? Do you pray and weep over the sheep? Are you tenderhearted and gentle with the people your husband pastors, or are you impatient, critical and indifferent toward those who might be a little difficult to lead? In all relationships, love is a choice!

Lessons on Love

I remember a time when God began dealing with my heart about loving His sheep, who according to my standard were not very lovable. Several years ago a new couple began visiting our church and soon joined our congregation. In the beginning they seemed zealous for God and excited about everything. But suddenly the wife (I will call her Sally) started fussing and nitpicking at almost every direction the church went. It seemed I was constantly on the phone or meeting with her to help undo her complicated thinking and bring understanding to her heart. It appeared that Sally thought she had more wisdom and knowledge to lead the church than her pastors. She seemed to feel comfortable—as well as justified—in her attempts to correct or rebuke her pastors for what she thought was our ignorance. And she simply could not understand why she did not get along with people. She insulted one person after another and would then call me on the telephone and cry, "I try to show myself friendly, but nooobody likes me!" It seemed like she was causing constant turmoil! If she was not crying because somebody had offended her, she was upset because someone was rejecting her! I found her behavior to be not only unbecoming, but also obnoxious and irritating!

One morning after spending half an hour of my time explaining to Sally why we were not going to handle a situation the way she thought we should, I thought her mind had finally clicked into reasonable gear and that she had laid down her argument. Two days later, however, I discovered that after hanging up the phone with me Sally had telephoned five other women to complain about the same issue! She had given each of them the same "yeah, but" arguments. And each of the women also had given her the same answers I had.

I was riding in the car with Karen, the director of our Pregnancy Care Center, when I discovered what had taken place with Sally. Karen had been one of the five women Sally had called. She probably would not have mentioned anything to me, except that Sally had told Karen she had also called the four other women, hoping someone would understand how she felt! Karen understood the potential division that was sown, and I appreciated her bringing it to my attention.

We were on our way to train new volunteers, and I was scheduled to teach on sharing the Gospel. Karen had asked me to begin training immediately after the women arrived, and I agreed. As we pulled into the parking lot, however, I spotted Sally's car. I was instantly reminded that Sally had been in training all week and would sit in my class. Still shocked by the "nerve of Sally," I bypassed irritation and went straight to infuriation! It felt like my spirit jerked within me at the very thought of seeing her, and my corrupt nature arose from the dead! My sweet little heart's desire suddenly changed from saving the lost to wanting to tell someone to get lost! Anger and disgust were all I could feel, and both of those feelings were aimed at Sally.

Even though I knew each of the five women Sally called had given her scriptural and godly answers, I could not help but wonder if there were others she might also have called. What if she had caused someone to stumble?

I asked for some time alone in my office before starting the class. When Karen asked me why, I said, "I need to pray! There is no way I can speak to those women until I get my heart right toward Sally." After hearing my answer and remembering Sally's difficult behavior in training all week, Karen quickly responded by asking if she could join me.

As soon as I entered my office and shut the door, I began pacing back and forth. There was no time to waste! People were waiting to be trained, and I really was not sure I would be able to move from anger to grace in such a short period of time. I knew that according to Scripture, I had to forgive Sally. I chose to do so, and then I began to pray.

"Father, forgive me for my anger! Forgive me for not loving Your sheep as You do. Forgive me for not handling this matter in a godly and mature fashion. Lord, give me Your heart and help me to respond toward Sally in the same manner that a loving mother would."

Immediately in my mind I saw a flock of sheep following me while I walked. When I looked back to see how they were doing, I noticed one little lamb had turned sideways and was trying to go in a different direction. Because the other sheep all were moving in one direction, the little lamb became stuck and hindered the rest of the sheep from following. I noticed that the little lamb was scrawny and unattractive and obviously needed special care and nourishment. With great compassion, I quickly ran toward the lamb and gently turned its body toward the right direction. I took time to give it special attention, lovingly stroking its bony back and petting its sweet little head. As I started to move forward again, however, the lamb turned to go astray, once more congesting the traffic flow for the rest of the sheep. After repeating this scenario a few times, my walk became more pronounced as I approached the lamb. Soon I was bending over quickly and grabbing its hind end, briskly turning it to face the right direction.

After having to correct the little lamb time after time, I became completely exasperated! In anger I marched toward the lamb and jerked it around, only this time I gave it a good, hard swat on the bottom!

Startled, the scrawny little lamb gave a pathetic, loud "baaaa!" and turned its head up to look at me. When I saw the face of this lamb, I started to laugh. It had Sally's face!

Immediately the Lord said, *She thinks she is a big, strong sheep, but she is really just a scrawny little lamb!*

My heart changed toward Sally at once, and instead of feeling angry toward her I began to bless her! First Samuel 13:14 tells us that King David had a heart after God's own heart and because of this God entrusted him to lead His people, the sheep of His pasture.

At that moment I realized how far I had fallen from having a heart after God's heart. But, oh, how I desired to understand the love and patience He has for His people!

Haven't we all, at one time or another, been like that scrawny little lamb, misguided by our own sense of direction and unaware of our slow pace of learning? Haven't there been times when we, too, were wise in our own eyes and just could not seem to move in the right direction? At some point in our walks with God, haven't most of us thought we were fully nourished, strong and mature because we were right in the middle of a people following after God?

Released in the love of God toward Sally, I dashed out of my office and headed toward the training session. I had a new and tender heart toward this precious lamb because God had enabled me to see her through His eyes. As a man on earth, Jesus was only able to do whatever He saw the Father doing (see John 5:19). If we are to be effective ministers, we must see what God is doing in the lives of people. Realizing that the Father had entrusted Sally to our care made me responsible to love her and to help lead her in the way of the Lord. If we love the Lord Jesus Christ, we will be more than happy to tend to His sheep and to feed them proper nourishment for spiritual growth (see John 21:15–21).

After entering the conference room and introducing myself to the class, I asked the women to go around the room and introduce themselves to me. When it was Sally's turn I was almost beaming with pride as I said, "I know Sally. She is a member of our congregation!"

As senior pastor of our church, my husband is responsible to watch out for the welfare of his flock. And as his wife who shares his heart, I am responsible for the welfare of the women in our church. I must choose to love them with the love of our Lord. Rather than being impatient, critical and indifferent toward those who might be a little difficult to lead, I must choose to be tenderhearted and gentle with each one. In so doing, I honor my husband and his ministry, and I honor the place where God has put me as a mother in the Kingdom.

I can confidently say that when my heart changed toward Sally, my husband was comforted, encouraged and honored!

Embracing the Father's Heart

God's main concern is souls. His heart beats: *Souls! Souls! Souls!* He cares deeply and affectionately about the welfare of every person. Our hearts must be found trustworthy regarding the things our Father cares about.

"The heart of her husband trusts in her confidently and relies on and believes in her securely. ... She comforts, encourages, and does him only good as long as there is life within her. ... [A]nd her husband boasts of and praises her" (Proverbs 31:11–12, 28). If we do not desire to embrace and walk after God's heart and passions, how can our husbands—who are called to impart God's heart and passion to others—trust in us? How can a husband expect his wife to do him only good—especially pertaining to God's call upon his life—if she does not help carry his burdens or encourage him to heed God's call? The atmospheres in our homes, lives and churches are affected by the decisions we make in our relational walks with both God and others.

"Be strong in the Lord [be empowered through your union with Him]; draw your strength from Him [that strength which His boundless might provides]" (Ephesians 6:10). The strength to do God's will is drawn from the very union we have with Him! By having and embracing the Father's heart and mind, we become empowered to stand against the fleshly emotions of anger, competition, jealousy or pride that try to rise up within us. Too often these feelings get in the way of loving people the way God does, and when our love grows dim, fear overshadows our hearts.

Standing Against Fear

In chapter 4, I mentioned that fear keeps women from ministry. Remember, there is no fear in love! God is love, and it is His love that frees us to do everything He has called us to do.

Satan is the enemy of your soul! This means that the devil hates you, is out to destroy you and has already declared war against you! His principal targets are the minds and emotions of God's children. He wants to instill fear in you! God's perfect love, however, not only heals all the past wounds of misunderstanding and rejection, but it also slams the door shut on fear and removes every trace of terror pertaining to both the devil and man!

"The fear of man brings a snare, but whoever leans on, trusts in, and puts his confidence in the Lord is safe and set on high" (Proverbs 29:25). The fear of man not only keeps women from ministry, but it also brings a *snare*—a trap, trick, pitfall or lure. The fear of man actually becomes something that entices and tempts us, catches and entangles us in sin in order to torment us! But as we put our confidence in the Lord, we become free from the lures that once entangled and tripped us, making us free to grow and develop in His love.

God's love frees us to love others in the same manner He loves us. The only fear we should know is the fear of the Lord, and it is good. It "leads to life" (Proverbs 19:23). It "brings instruction in Wisdom" (Proverbs 15:33). It "is the beginning of Wisdom and skill" (Psalm 111:10). "It will be well with those who [reverently] fear God" (Ecclesiastes 8:12). "The reward of humility and the reverent and worshipful fear of the Lord is riches and honor and life" (Proverbs 22:4). It "prolongs one's days" (Proverbs 10:27). And it "is clean" (Psalm 19:9).

A woman cannot be held back from happiness or from accomplishing God's will when she walks in the fear of the Lord!

Her husband will see this and will boast of and praise her, saying, "Many daughters have done virtuously, nobly, and well [with the strength of character that is steadfast in goodness], but you excel them all. Charm and grace are deceptive, and beauty is vain [because it is not lasting], but a woman who reverently and worshipfully fears the Lord, she shall be praised!" (Proverbs 31:29–30).

The Husband Has Power, Too

And so we see in this passage from Proverbs that the husband has great power as well. Although at times he may feel helpless in protecting his wife, he can pave the way of respect and ministry for his wife by publicly validating and honoring her. If he consistently lifts her up, then her soul will be healed and she will be established alongside the work he is doing. Before long, the people will recognize her love and valuable ministry to them. The church will see them as a team, much like children recognize their own father and mother. I have never heard anyone refer to their biological parents as my "father and his wife" but only as my "father and mother." To children, parents always come as a pair and are one unit!

A good husband exalts his wife in their home. He shares the leadership of the family with her. He considers her counsel, makes decisions with her and demands respect for her from their children. I believe God ordained the husband/wife team to have one heart, mind and calling—just as He did His Church.

United in Purpose

God instructs us in His Word on how to live and function with one another:

[Living as becomes you] with complete lowliness of mind (humility) and meekness (unselfishness, gentleness, mildness), with patience, bearing with one another and making allowances because you love one another. Be eager and strive earnestly to guard and keep the harmony and oneness of [and produced by] the Spirit in the binding power of peace. [There is] one body and one Spirit—just as there is also one hope [that belongs] to the calling you received—[There is] one Lord, one faith, one baptism, One God and Father of [us] all, Who is above all [Sovereign over all], pervading all and [living] in [us] all.

Ephesians 4:2–6

The apostle Paul wrote this concerning the Church. But these words also pertain to the family. When Paul spoke concerning the family and its order, he said, "This mystery is very great, but I speak concerning [the relation of] Christ and the church" (Ephesians 5:32).

In our churches, as well as in our homes, we obviously have different functions. Even though a man has the ability to do most of the same type of work a woman does and a woman can do the work a man can do, she cannot function as a father nor he as a mother. When operating in their God-given roles they both minister love, truth and encouragement to the family. I am convinced that both ministries are needed, and without this balance both the family and Church will experience lack—and be dysfunctional!

The couples who are united together in purpose and vision operate in true teamwork. They build one another up and encourage each other for the tasks set before them. Together they are strengthened in the joy of the Lord as they take pleasure in the things God has anointed them to do. These couples never stand alone, but in their own marriages and ministries they walk out Romans 12:15–16 and Galatians 6:2:

Rejoice with those who rejoice [sharing others' joy]; and weep with those who weep [sharing others' grief]. Live in harmony with one another; do not be haughty (snobbish, high-minded, exclusive), but readily adjust yourself to [people, things] and give yourselves to humble tasks. Never overestimate yourself or be wise in your own conceits.

Bear (endure, carry) one another's burdens and troublesome moral faults, and in this way fulfill and observe perfectly the law of Christ (the Messiah), and complete what is lacking [in your obedience to it].

These are the couples God can use to transform His Kingdom!

It Is Time to Go On!

"I am convinced and sure of this very thing, that He Who began a good work in you will continue until the day of Jesus Christ [right up to the time of His return], developing [that good work] and perfecting and bringing it to full completion in you" (Philippians 1:6).

To the pastors' wives reading this, I tell you:

Perhaps in the past you have been wounded and held back by the lies of the enemy. Perhaps you have resented having to live your life in a fishbowl, and because of this you have been uninvolved in your husband's ministry. Today the Father is calling you to repent and change your mind from past thinking. It is not too late to start fresh and new. As you walk in the fear of the Lord, God's wisdom will take hold of you and honor will follow you. God wants to take you out of brokenness and spiritual barrenness and raise you up to a place of spiritual motherhood within His Kingdom. He has called you to teach the younger women through word and example that everything pertaining to life and godliness is met through Christ Jesus.

Like it or not, if your husband is sitting in the gate of spiritual authority, then your behavior, actions and reactions toward God, His plans, His people and your husband are going to affect the younger women in your church. They are looking for an example, and their eyes are upon you! They see you as a mother, a mentor and a friend. How you see yourself does not determine how they see you. Your life will teach them, whether it be right or wrong behavior! God has called you to help your husband care for the souls of mankind. He has called you to be an example of submission and respect.

Submission is a word often hated and misunderstood by women. Yet when we break down the meaning of the word, we are able to understand both the privilege and power given to a woman submitting to her husband.

Sub: under or underling, meaning help.

Mission: assignment, task, purpose, duty and commission.

Submission simply means to come under the mission to which your husband is called, and then help him in it. What a privilege, what an honor and what a calling!

It is the calling of a mother in the Kingdom.

10

Daughters, Arise!

THE NEWS MEDIA constantly report on national debt, school shootings, terrorism and chemical warfare. They tell of pestilence and disease, earthquakes, wars and rumors of wars (see Matthew 24). These evidences that we are walking in the final days can threaten and immobilize some people with hopelessness and fear!

God's Word tells us, however, that the Church is not to cower in fear. We are to arise when great darkness covers the earth, and as we do the glory of the Lord will shine brightly from our lives. "Arise [from the depression and prostration in which circumstances have kept you—rise to a new life]! Shine (be radiant with the glory of the Lord), for your light has come, and the glory of the Lord is risen upon you!" (Isaiah 60:1). In this urgent hour God's people must make His saving power known to mankind, and we must prepare for what He is going to do on this earth through us!

I feel a sense of special urgency for His daughters to step up to holy and dedicated living. Women need to be gathered, mentored and released to live and function in God's anointing as they are brought into the Kingdom in these end times. Now is the time to prepare ourselves in righteous living. Now is the time to be harvesters. Now is the time to increase our level of faith, and now is the time to do the Father's work!

Now is the time to *arise*!

Appointed for Such a Time as This

Queen Esther was brought into her position at a specific time for a specific purpose. She arose to her calling and saved her nation, which had been doomed to destruction. Because of her wisdom and humility God exalted Esther. (I expound on the character of Esther in my book *Women of Royalty*.) Esther 8:5–8 says that because the king's heart trusted in her, Esther was given an irreversible authority! The Word also reveals that after the king gave his authority to his bride, it brought new hope, gladness, joy and honor to the people. Many people were converted, and God's people ruled powerfully over their enemies (see Esther 8:16–17).

Just like Esther, we have been brought into the Kingdom for such a time as this. God is calling His daughters to participate in and for His purposes. Sometimes we see ourselves as insignificant misfits or orphans who received pity and grace like Esther did. We sometimes forget that God has raised us up, too, and has brought us into the Kingdom to rule and reign with the King.

God longs to place the crown of His favor upon us and to put His ring on our hands so we can rule with irreversible authority! As we pursue the King and His ways for our lives, we will experientially know the favor of God. Because His love expands in us, the desire to see His Kingdom come will move us to serve, as Esther did, as mothers in God's Kingdom and to intercede for the salvation of mankind.

I Must Occupy!

After ministering for eleven days and nights at the Women of Destiny convention in Uyo, Nigeria, as well as at a local Bible college, I looked forward to a relaxing two-hour flight back to Lagos. The airline on which I was scheduled to travel was known for its excellence. It had air conditioning—a luxury I really looked forward to!—and was fully serviced.

As we headed toward the airport, my escort informed me he had lost my airline ticket. Nevertheless, he guaranteed me a flight to Lagos. He promised that a new ticket would be bought for me when we arrived at the airport and I was "not to worry!"

After arriving at the terminal, my escort entered a small, enclosed glass room. I could see him arguing with an airline official. When he saw me watching him, my escort smiled and gave me a signal that all was well. Finally he came out of the room with a ticket to Lagos. Soon afterward I waved good-bye and boarded the plane.

I found my assigned seat and sat down. But when I leaned into my seat it fell backward, and I almost landed in the person's lap behind me! I quickly apologized and then moved into the next seat beside a man at the window. I muttered something like, "I hope this seat is not assigned to someone else." The man assured me that it was not, and I wondered how he knew.

I kept wondering when the service would begin. For almost the first hour of flight, I waited for drinks to be served. I was getting hot and uncomfortable and thought, "Great! The air conditioning is broken." Not only was the air not working, but also the air vents above my seat and the seat next to me were broken. Later I discovered the new flight arrangement my escort had made for me was with an airline that was known to "go down [crash] daily"!

After an hour of flying, the plane began to land. I asked the man next to me if we had already arrived in Lagos. He smiled and said, "No, the plane is dropping off passengers and picking up new passengers." He strongly advised me to stay in my seat!

I watched as several passengers left the plane. Then after several people boarded, the door was shut quickly and forcefully. Suddenly two children started crying and a hysterical woman began yelling. I was told that the flight had been overbooked and some of the people who were waiting to board were left outside, including the mother of the two crying children. Apparently the mother's friend ushered the children into the plane, and the mother was tailing behind when the door closed. The people on the plane began to command the stewards to let in the mother. The pilot came out and tried to reason with the people. He explained that the plane had a seating limit and was full. But the people would not settle down, so he decided to open the door to let the mother onto the airplane.

The moment the door opened, the angry mob on the other side pushed through and burst onto the plane. They began scrambling for seats. It was obvious there were not enough seats for all of us. An immediate fight broke out with arguments concerning the danger of an overloaded airplane. Men and women were yelling, crying and pushing one another up and down the aisle.

The air was so hot and stuffy that I really thought I might die! Finally I yelled, "You don't understand! If the plane is over-loaded, it will go down!"

You could hear a pin drop as everyone looked at the only white face and foreigner on the plane. I thought, "Not a good move, Shirley!" I quickly looked down to the floor and quietly prayed that I would not be thrown off.

A tall and distinguished man ran to take the seat that origi-nally had been assigned to me. Of course, he immediately fell backward. I looked at him apologetically and said, "I am sorry, but that seat is broken." The man quickly placed his arm behind the back of his seat and with a hard jerk pulled it to an upright position. Holding his seat, he looked at me and said, "I must occupy!"

I promptly nodded and replied, "You must occupy!"

This man was not about to allow his seat to be taken away! In order to get where he was going, he had to occupy that seat. He was aggressive because he had an agenda that he was deter-mined to meet. He refused to miss his opportunity to seize his destination. When brokenness affected his life, he was willing to hold and support it for the entire journey.

As God's daughters and citizens in His Kingdom, we can learn a lot from this Nigerian man. We have a purpose and a mandate to fulfill. Isn't it time for us to enthusiastically seize our destinies? Isn't it time to stop letting brokenness hinder our pursuit and instead lift it up to God? Isn't it time to become strong? Shouldn't we be willing to give up our rights for the journey and instead strengthen and support others? Isn't it time to declare, "I must occupy," and then move forward in God's purposes? Remember, the violent take as a precious prize the Kingdom by force (see Matthew 11:12).

If a door closes before us, isn't it time to knock and keep knocking, pressing in until we break through into the fullness of what God has for us (see Matthew 7:7–8)? God wants us to aggressively persevere until we have broken through every obstacle. He will be our strength!

Being Occupied with Our Father's Business

When Jesus was twelve years old, He went up with His parents to Jerusalem for Passover. When the feast ended, their caravan left and traveled a day's journey before His parents realized Jesus was not with them. Frantically they returned to Jerusalem looking for their son, and after three days they found Him in the court of the Temple. Jesus had been sitting among the teachers where He was listening and asking questions. All who had heard His questions were "astonished and overwhelmed with bewildered wonder at His intelligence and understanding and His replies" (Luke 2:47).

When His mother asked Jesus why He had caused His parents to worry, Jesus was surprised that they did not know where He would be! Jesus answered, "It is necessary [as a duty] for Me to be in My Father's house and [occupied] about My Father's business" (Luke 2:49).

Jesus also has told us, His people, to "occupy" until He comes through a parable about a nobleman who went to a far country to receive a kingdom for himself. In this parable, the nobleman gave wages to his citizens before he left. He told them he would return to rule and reign, but while he was gone he wanted them to stay busy, working hard until he returned. When the nobleman came back, he discovered that some of the citizens had worked diligently and had increased what they had been given. The master was delighted and declared that they were good and faithful! Because they had proven their loyalty and faithfulness to this nobleman, he gave them authority to rule and reign with him in his Kingdom.

One man, however, despised his leadership. He sat idly and did not develop or use what had been given to him. Instead he hid what he had because he was lazy and rebellious. When the nobleman discovered what this servant had done, he was angry! The nobleman took back what little he had given this man and gave it to another who had been faithful (see Luke 19:12–27).

God wants to multiply the works of our hands! If we hide what He has given us, then He will take what has been hidden and give it to those who are faithful. More than anything, God wants us to love Him and to have the same passion for His Kingdom that He has. If we will diligently develop and cultivate His love in the fields of this world, then the work of our hands will bring forth a mighty harvest of souls.

Just like Jesus was "occupied" with His Father's business when His parents went looking for Him, so God wants to find us occupied with His work. To the degree we are faithful and loyal to Him and His purposes, to that same degree God will release His authority to us to rule and reign with Him.

Parable of the Ten Virgins

Christ is returning for a pure and spotless Bride who is prepared for His coming. Jesus said:

175

The kingdom of heaven shall be likened to ten virgins who took their lamps and went to meet the bridegroom. Five of them were foolish (thoughtless, without forethought) and five were wise (sensible, intelligent, and prudent). For when the foolish took their lamps, they did not take any [extra] oil with them; But the wise took flasks of oil along with them [also] with their lamps. While the bridegroom lingered and was slow in coming, they all began nodding their heads, and they fell asleep. But at midnight there was a shout, Behold, the bridegroom! Go out to meet him! Then all those virgins got up and put their own lamps in order. And the foolish said to the wise, Give us some of your oil, for our lamps are going out. But the wise replied, There will not be enough for us and for you; go instead to the dealers and buy for yourselves. But while they were going away to buy, the bridegroom came, and those who were prepared went in with him to the marriage feast; and the door was shut. Later the other virgins also came, and said, Lord, Lord, open [the door] to us! But He replied, I solemnly declare to you, I do not know you [I am not acquainted with you]. Watch therefore [give strict attention and be cautious and active], for you know neither the day nor the hour when the Son of Man will come.

Matthew 25:1–13

In this parable Jesus is referring to His Church, the Bride of Christ. She is made up of individual believers who become one through their united hearts. Though they all have been given lamps that contain light, each individual is responsible for his or her own actions and to remain filled. While these words refer to God's Church as a whole, they have a very special meaning for His daughters, because the idea of being His Bride is quite close to our hearts.

But what specifically can we women do to prepare for His coming? How can we ensure that our lamps are full and we are ready for the Bridegroom's arrival? What can we do to better serve as mothers in the Kingdom of God, mentoring spiritual daughters to help them develop into women of power and to prepare them for Christ's return?

Clothe Yourself with Wisdom

I believe the first thing we must do is clothe ourselves with wisdom. Let's consider two questions concerning the parable of the virgins:

1. Did the foolish virgins believe the groom was coming less than the wise virgins believed he was coming?
2. Did the foolish virgins look forward to or anticipate his coming less than the wise virgins?

The answer to both these questions, of course, is *No!* What then is the difference between the two groups of virgins? The only difference is their degree of wisdom.

The Amplified Bible describes the foolish virgins as thoughtless and without forethought. They were so busy with the cares of life that they forgot how important it was to keep their lamps filled with oil. Their lackadaisical attitude is symbolic of the lukewarm Church that is satisfied with a touch of God's presence, rather than with His fullness.

The wise virgins, on the other hand, are described as sensible, intelligent and prudent. To be *prudent* means to be "cautious and to think carefully before doing something." Their wisdom is what prepared them for the return of the bridegroom.

Wisdom is the comprehensive insight into God's ways and purposes and is found throughout God's Word. The book of Proverbs, for example, was written "that people may know skillful and godly Wisdom and instruction, discern and comprehend the words of understanding and insight, Receive instruction in wise dealing and the discipline of wise thoughtfulness, righteousness, justice, and integrity, That prudence may be given to the simple, and knowledge, discretion, and discernment to the youth" (Proverbs 1:2–4). If we will receive God's words and be attentive to skillful and godly wisdom, if we will seek her as silver and search for her in the same way we would search for hidden treasure, then wisdom will enter our hearts, discretion shall watch over us and understanding will keep us—to deliver us (see Proverbs 2).

I want to embrace wisdom that displays forethought in preparation for our Groom. We women need to watch carefully how we walk, to be ever filled with the Spirit of God and to diligently occupy—serving Him until He comes! The wisdom of God will keep us alert to watch carefully so that our light does not become darkness (see Luke 11:34–36).

Exemplifying His Bride

The second thing we must do to prepare spiritual daughters for Christ's return is to be living examples of the Bride of Christ. Women who are married have had to learn to function in our God-given roles as brides and wives. Thus, our very existence as women has empowered us to serve in the future of God's Kingdom! Because of this we have a responsibility to share what we have learned (and are still learning) with the rest of the Church. We are in a unique position to be a holy demonstration of what it means to be Christ's Bride and helpmate.

If women will "walk (lead a life) worthy of the [divine] calling to which you have been called [with behavior that is a credit to the summons to God's service, Living as becomes you] with complete lowliness of mind (humility) and meekness (unselfishness, gentleness, mildness), with patience, bearing with one another and making allowances because you love one another," if we will "be eager and strive earnestly to guard and keep the harmony and oneness of [and produced by] the Spirit in the binding power of peace" (Ephesians 4:1–3), then we will exemplify Christ's Body and illustrate with our lives the function and behavior of His Bride.

The happiest and most effective marriages are those in which the husband and wife share the same heartbeat and passion for the vision and purposes to which they are called. In the same manner, Christ is coming back for a Bride who is devoted as much to the Father's purposes as He is. She will be up and about her Father's business as well.

One day Christ will display His Bride as glorious! Her heart will thrill at the look of pleasure in His eyes as He beholds her beauty and says, "Many . . . have done virtuously, . . . but you excel them all!" (Proverbs 31:29).

Prepare Our Own Lives

The third thing we must do to prepare others for the return of our Lord is to prepare our own lives for His coming. Christ is not coming back for a Bride who is slothful and depressed or has done nothing to prepare herself for His return, but whose appearance is beautiful and perfect in righteousness. The clothing she wears is gracious behavior belonging to Christ. Having once been cleansed by His blood, she steadily removes spots reflecting her old nature with the washing of the Word. Having been pressed by heated trials, imperfect wrinkles of self-centeredness and inhibitions are removed. She takes great care not to allow self-ishness or cowardly fears to crease or fold her garment again.

This Bride will not keep her house (life) a mess, and she will not clutter it with unnecessary stuff. Her home will shine in the uncompromising order of His will. Christ's Bride will be excited and vivacious about the future and will expectantly anticipate His presence, as well as their habitation together. Because of her commitment and intense love for her Husband, the simple pleasure of bringing joy to His heart will be what delights and motivates her from day to day.

Be Carriers of His Authority and Presence

The fourth thing women must do to prepare others for the return of our Lord is to serve as living examples of His authority and power. In the early days of the Church as documented in the book of Acts, the Spirit of the Lord came with a sound like a mighty rushing wind (see Acts 2:2), tongues of fire appeared over each head (see Acts 2:3), the building shook because the people were united in prayer (see Acts 4:31) and signs and wonders began to permeate the works of the followers of Christ. "And they went out and preached everywhere, while the Lord kept working with them and confirming the message by the attesting signs and miracles that closely accompanied [it]" (Mark 16:20). The Church today marvels at such a miraculous picture, thinking, *No wonder the early Church was dedicated to her belief in Christ!* But those things happened *because* they believed in Christ and were dedicated to Him, and there is no reason why those types of things cannot happen today.

So why don't we see more such signs and wonders? Personally, I have some nifty ideas why God might be holding back, but in truth I really do not know for sure! I do know one thing, though: My faith has been increasing as I have seen an increase of signs and wonders awaking the Church's passion for God and His purposes. I am beginning to believe God really can do anything He wants to do for whatever reason He wants to do it, and whenever He wants to do it! God does show His approval by signs, wonders and various miraculous manifestations of His power (see Hebrews 2:4).

Signs and wonders reveal the reality of God to those who have not believed. These wonders cannot be explained or reasoned away but are a powerful evidence of God's presence. Shouldn't we expect supernatural manifestations of His presence when people—who have the Spirit of God dwelling within them—gather in unity to worship God and pray? Isn't Jesus Christ the same today as He was yesterday and will be forever (see Hebrews 13:8)? Ceasing to be amazed in His presence is a sign that we have been taking Him for granted!

We ought to expect to see His power manifested through us! We ought to be speaking with the authority of God Himself!

Ah, but therein lies the problem. Where is the authority? The Church has seen some power and gifts in operation, but very little authority has been seen upon God's people.

If a woman truly loves her husband, she would not think of abusing or usurping his authority. And because she respects and honors him, he desires to release his authority to her. In the same manner, authority will be given to those God trusts because they have been found faithful to what His heart values.

This is where we women must serve as examples. We can operate in His authority *if* we are found faithful to what *His* heart values. Jesus said that many are called, but only a few are chosen (see Matthew 20:16). The reason for this is simply because only a few are willing to pay the price of complete abandonment to His will. God is looking for total surrender to Him, so that He can trust us to carry His presence to the world. When this happens, new vision and liberty also will come upon us. We will exhibit bravery to the enemy and display God's glory through signs and wonders.

No matter what your life was like in the past, God's purpose is for you to serve Him today. Remember Mary Magdalene? Jesus delivered her from seven demons that controlled and tormented her life, and afterward she served God from a grateful heart. So devoted was she to the Gospel of Christ that she became the first one commissioned to preach the Gospel concerning His resurrection (see Matthew 27:56–61; Mark 15:40; Luke 8:2; 24:10; and John 19:25; 20:1–18)! She loved Him deeply and was thoroughly devoted to His purposes. God not only forgave Mary's sins, but because she was faithful He gave her authority.

The Lord is longing to release authority to His Bride. When He does, she will have great power over the evil one. When she speaks, blind eyes will see, deaf ears will open and the dead will be raised!

May our prayer to God be: "Gird Your sword upon Your thigh, O mighty One, in Your glory and Your majesty! And in Your majesty ride on triumphantly for the cause of truth, humility, and righteousness (uprightness and right standing with God); and let Your right hand guide You to tremendous things" (Psalm 45:3–4).

May we carry His presence to display His glory as He does great things through us!

Destroy the "D" Darts of the Devil

Once we become carriers of His authority, we must begin to operate in the fifth thing that God wants us to do in order to prepare others for His Son's return. We must know how to resist our enemy. God wants to demonstrate His power to others through you and me just like He did through Jesus, but first we must learn to destroy the works of the devil in our own lives.

The apostle John said, "The reason the Son of God was made manifest (visible) was to undo (destroy, loosen, and dissolve) the works the devil [has done]" (1 John 3:8).

In numerous places throughout this book I have touched on the role the enemy plays in our lives. As followers of Christ and soldiers in His Kingdom, it is vital that we recognize a war is raging, and it is not going to diminish. Instead, it is only going to intensify. Our adversary has a strategy in his warfare against us, so our first step is to recognize his deceits so we can foil his plans. First Peter 5:8 says, "Be well-balanced (temperate, sober of mind), be vigilant and cautious at all times; for that enemy of yours, the devil, roams around like a lion roaring [in fierce hunger], seeking someone to seize upon and devour."

The devil throws what I call **"D" Darts** at us to hinder our pursuit of God. These **Debilitating** darts are designed to weaken us, handicap us, dilute our work and make us ineffective. They are **Diversions** and **Distractions** and are intended to turn our focus away from God's vision and purposes. These subtle darts capitalize on everyday circumstances and feelings. They are not fatal but are intended to wound, weaken and slow down our pace until we are spiritually immobilized. If we tolerate our enemy's efforts and do not counterattack with God's Word, then

183

the devil will succeed at hindering and dividing Christ's Bride from her strength and unity.

Let's take a look at the enemy's "D" dart strategy:

When difficult circumstances come, the devil throws darts of **Disappointment** our way. Choosing to walk in disappointment rather than putting our hope in God slows down our pace.

Then about the time we recognize that this slower pace has hindered our passion, he flings **Discouragement** at our hearts. Discouragement now makes it difficult to praise God.

The devil capitalizes on this struggle and throws another dart: **Depression.** This affects every aspect of our lives!

Recognizing his accomplishment, Satan aims for our faith with **Doubt.**

Because everything in which we have put our trust has been shaken by unbelief, the devil then catches us off guard and strikes our joy with **Despair.**

When **Dissatisfaction** pierces our hearts, Satan hits us hard with **Discontentment.**

Now, almost every time we speak, darts of **Dissension** from our hearts are spoken by our own mouths as we sow darts of **Discord**!

The stage is then set for great **Division,** and because of this **Distrust** runs rampant!

Then the devil starts the same cycle over again! Because our hearts cannot trust, we feel so **Disappointed.** . . .

So how do we withstand the devil's "D" darts? How do we withstand him if we are weak? We draw our strength from our union with Christ. Through our intimacy with Him, we are made strong against the wiles of the devil.

> Be strong in the Lord [be empowered through your union with Him]; draw your strength from Him [that strength which His boundless might provides]. Put on God's whole armor [the armor of a heavy-armed soldier which God supplies], that you may be able successfully to stand up against [all] the strategies and the deceits of the devil.
>
> Ephesians 6:10–11

> Withstand him; be firm in faith [against his onset—rooted, established, strong, immovable, and determined], knowing that the same (identical) sufferings are appointed to your brotherhood (the whole body of Christians) throughout the world. And after you have suffered a little while, the God of all grace [Who imparts all blessing and favor], Who has called you to His [own] eternal glory in Christ Jesus, will Himself complete and make you what you ought to be, establish and ground you securely, and strengthen, and settle you.
>
> 1 Peter 5:9–10

Embrace Love

The sixth thing we women must do to prepare for our Lord is to embrace His love for His children. Several years ago I met a precious woman while ministering with my husband in another country. She had a strong desire to minister to women but considered herself to be deficient in wisdom, knowledge and practical experience. I looked at this woman who had eight

185

children and asked if she knew everything about being a mother before she became one. She laughed and said, "No!"

I told her that I had been observing her while I stayed in her home and saw how well she managed her family. Not only was she an excellent mother to her small children, but she also had trained her older daughters to help care for the little ones—and they were good at what they did!

"What enabled you to become such an excellent mother?" I asked. "You said you did not have a clue how to begin. Did you find yourself learning day by day along the way?"

As she began to connect what I was saying with ministry to others, I asked, "What motivated you to hold your little ones, feed them, clean up after them and teach them right from wrong?"

"Love!" she declared with wide eyes and a big smile.

"That's how simple it will be to obey God's call on your life. Just embrace love," I said.

We will learn how to minister to God's people as we love Him and the people He sends our way. The more we love Him, the more we will seek after Him to know and understand His ways. The more we seek after Him, the more we will find Him and the fullness of His purposes. The more we find Him, the more He will fill us with Himself. The more He fills us with Himself, the more empowered we will be to display His attributes. He is our sufficiency and might, and we can do all things through Him!

Proverbs 31 describes the making of a valuable wife or a wife who is high in excellence as one who continually gives of herself. She is also known for her love, and because of this she is highly productive. Every great woman of God came out of smallness, brokenness, bondage or hiding. His plan is for us to develop into the fullness of His love, gather others into His Kingdom and reproduce faithful sons and daughters of the Most High.

186

Don't be satisfied with being unproductive in these last days. God is a great God!

Live a Sacrificial Life

The final thing we must do to prepare for Christ's return—and the thing that perhaps encompasses all the others in a nutshell—is to live a life separated unto Him.

The apostle Paul begged the Roman Christians to live a sacrificial life that was holy, devoted and consecrated to the Lord. He explained that this was only a reasonable response to the great love and sacrifice Christ has bestowed upon us. If we will yield our lives to God, as Paul beseeched us to do, then our human thinking will be replaced by new ideas and attitudes, transforming our behavior and character into the image of Christ.

> Do not be conformed to this world (this age), [fashioned after and adapted to its external, superficial customs], but be transformed (changed) by the [entire] renewal of your mind [by its new ideals and its new attitude], so that you may prove [for yourselves] what is the good and acceptable and perfect will of God, even the thing which is good and acceptable and perfect [in His sight for you].
>
> Romans 12:2

Have you been caught up in this world's passions and frustrations? Living a life separated unto God will bring peace, joy and contentment, and this kind of service and spiritual worship will produce perfection in your life concerning God's will.

God Wants to Make a Big Mama Out of You!

Women ministers in Nigeria are called *Mama*. I found this term of respect very sweet when I arrived there for a women's convention. The day before the conference began, my daughter and I were taken to our room and asked to stay there until someone came to get us. We waited while several pastors who were involved in the convention met to pray and discuss the coming event. I was told that at the proper time I would be presented and introduced to these leaders.

The door finally opened, and we were led into the meeting room. At once, all the pastors stood and bowed respectfully as each one welcomed me.

"Oh, Mama, you are so welcome!"

"We have been praying for these meetings, and Mama, God has shown us that He will do great and mighty things through you."

"We shall see miracles and signs and wonders, Mama!"

"Thank you, Mama, for coming."

I was not accustomed to such faith or respect. I opened my mouth and said, "Umm . . . excuse me, God can do anything He wants to do, but it is important that you understand something. . . . I am just an ordinary woman."

One of the pastors abruptly corrected what I was saying: "Do not say you are ordinary, Mama. God has sent you to us, and we shall see great things, Mama! No, we will *not* call you Mama. We shall call you *Big Mama!*"

They seemed surprised when my daughter almost fell over laughing! I quickly apologized, however, and told him he was right. Even though I may not be much in myself, a great big God lives inside me, and He can do whatever He wants to do.

Arise!

I hear God asking, "Where are My Big Mamas? Where are My mighty ones? Where are My intercessors? Where are My mothers of faith?

"Where are My Sarahs? My Deborahs? My Jaels? Where are My Naomis, Ruths and Hannahs? Where are My Esthers, Abigails and Jehoshebas? Where are My Priscillas and Marys?"

God wants to make Big Mamas out of His daughters. He is looking for mothers in the Kingdom to arise. In these last days He wants to enlarge Himself in each one of us.

As ambassadors of our Father, the King, our purpose is to represent Jesus Christ so the world might be brought to salvation through Him. He wants us to perform His works and victory! He wants to reveal His glory through us! If we will tap into the potential for which God created us, it will blow our minds! As God's life is made active through us, we will perform the works of Christ and free people from the snares and bondage of sin, just as Christ did. His vision will keep us going in purpose, keep us motivated in zeal and keep us energetic and productive! Because of this, the Church will be empowered to display God's magnificent glory! Remember, God will do far above and beyond what we could ever dream, think or imagine!

Are you ready to serve as a mother in the Kingdom of God? Are you ready to be a Sarah, a Deborah, a Jael, a Naomi or Ruth, an Esther, Abigail or Jehosheba, a Priscilla or Mary? Are you willing to be a Big Mama? If you are, He will use you to the fulfillment of His purposes and to the completion of His harvest. He will reveal His glory through you so that you can say along with Hannah:

There is none holy like the Lord, there is none besides You; there is no Rock like our God. . . . [T]he Lord is a God of knowledge, and by Him actions are weighed. The bows of the mighty are broken, and those who stumbled are girded with strength. Those who were full have hired themselves out for bread, but those who were hungry have ceased to hunger. The barren has borne seven, but she who has many children languishes and is forlorn. The Lord slays and makes alive; He brings down to Sheol and raises up. The Lord makes poor and makes rich; He brings low and He lifts up. He raises up the poor out of the dust and lifts up the needy from the ash heap, to make them sit with the nobles, and inherit the throne of glory. For the pillars of the earth are the Lord's, and He has set the world upon them. He will guard the feet of His godly ones, but the wicked shall be silenced and perish in darkness; for by strength shall no man prevail. The adversaries of the Lord shall be broken to pieces; against them will He thunder in heaven. The Lord will judge [all peoples] to the ends of the earth; and He will give strength to His king (King) and exalt the power of His anointed (Anointed His Christ).

1 Samuel 2:2–10

Father, Make Us What We Ought to Be

Father, You have called us to love and nurture the harvest to come. You have called us to diligently teach those who are being gathered to Your house to both love and fear Your name. You have given us a mandate to live righteously and to carry Your glory as we demonstrate Your attributes with signs and wonders.

Father, we are willing to serve as mothers in Your Kingdom. We call upon You to strengthen, complete and perfect us so

190

that we can fulfill this role with Your infilling, Your grace and Your love. Make us what we ought to be and equip us with every good thing, so that we might carry out Your will and serve You as effective mothers in Your Kingdom. We ask that You work in us to accomplish what is pleasing in Your sight through Jesus Christ.

To You be the glory forever and ever. Amen (see Hebrews 13:21)!

Shirley Sustar is founder of Women of Royalty Ministries and author of *Women of Royalty*. She serves alongside her husband, Jim, who is senior pastor of Heartland Christian Center in Wooster, Ohio. They have been married 38 years and have four children ranging from 19 to 33 years of age and six grandchildren. Shirley looks *much* younger than she sounds.

Along with ministering outside her local congregation in the U.S. and abroad, Shirley actively leads the women's ministry of Heartland Christian Center, training teams of women to teach, counsel, direct and care for other women. She also is on the advisory board for the Pregnancy Care Center of Wayne County, where she once directed the Post Abortion Counseling Ministry. Shirley has a love for the prophetic and a passion to see people recognize and rise to their full potential in Christ Jesus (see Isaiah 60:1–3).

You may contact Shirley Sustar at:

Women of Royalty Ministries
(330) 345-6780
WORoyalty@aol.com